COMMUNICATING:

A Pastor's Job

Volume 2: Situations

Robert D. Kendall
MDiv. PhD.

BOBALU Publications
St.Cloud, Minnesota

Communicating: A Pastor's Job
Volume 2: Situations

Published by BOBALU Publications
2578 14 1/2 Avenue SE St. Cloud, MN 56304

ISBN 0-9647-504-1-4

First Edition

Cover Design: Nancy Jean Schram
Printing: Sentinel Printing, St. Cloud, MN

Table of Contents

A Special Acknowledgment

Volume One acknowledged my debt to my wife, LuBell, and to my four children—all who helped me discover who I am and who supported me far beyond my deserving in my quest to understand this phenomenon called "communication."

In this Companion Volume, I wish to acknowledge some other people who have contributed greatly to my understanding of life in general and to communication in particular: my colleagues in the clergy and my colleagues in the Speech Communication Department at St. Cloud State University.

In the clergy, I wish to acknowledge my colleagues in the pastorate in three different conferences (areas) of the United Methodist Church: those I served with as a young man in the ministry in Northern New York; those I served with in rural ministry in North Iowa; and those I have served with in various cities and towns of the Minnesota Conference. These are special people who often go unrecognized, but who perform their ministry in many faithful ways; and, in doing so, become models for Christ-like living.

My teaching colleagues are special people, too. For twenty-one years, we struggled together to build the Speech Communication Department into one of the very best in the nation. In our relating, we learned much about the subject we had chosen to teach. In our teaching, we learned to respect each other's abilities and contributions as we determined to bring the very best instruction to our students. I especially want to acknowledge my debt to three of my colleagues: Chuck Vick, Art Grachek, and Don Sikkink.

Each one of these men taught me some valuable lessons in human communication. However, it is their friendship that I most value. And for that I am very thankful. I hope these two volumes will not be an embarrassment to them, and that much of what I have written will be understood by them as an extension of their teaching into another vocation so dependent on communication.

Preface

This Companion Volume begins with Chapter Ten because it is an extension of Volume One. The Situations in which a pastor communicates rightly follows an understanding of the Basics of communication.

As with the first volume, I have approached the second from an interpersonal communication perspective, applying its discoveries and ideosyncracies to common pastoral situations. I continue, at the beginning of each chapter, to identify Scriptural passages (from the New Revised Standard Version) which illustrate some aspect of the chapter's subject, using them as examples of a specific situation in which communication occurs and as springboards into the discussion. Each one of the first four chapters focuses on a particular situation common in most pastorates—situations with which all pastors are well acquainted: informal conversations; interpersonal relationships; small groups, particularly committees; and public speaking, particularly preaching. Chapter Fourteen attempts to shed some light on four different situations which often cause a pastor some amount of frustration and/or anxiety: power differences; communicating within the organization; male/female communication; and family relationships. The final chapter focuses on the subject of ethics in communication, as an aid in better understanding one's own behavior plus the communication behavior of the laypeople whom we serve and with whom we minister.

When I first decided to write *Communicating: A Pastor's Job*, I was responding more to the stated concerns of the laity as I was hearing them speak and complain, than I was to the recognized needs of the pastoral clergy. Over the years, I have been in the position to hear layperson after layperson say, upon learning that I was a Professor of Speech Communication, "I wish you could teach our pastor to communicate better. S/he's a wonderful person, but has trouble communicating in this or that situation." They're either a good preacher and a poor conversationalist, an effective worker in small groups but terrible in maintaining a relationship, or any number of combinations. Seldom did I hear "Our pastor is a great communicator, in whatever situation s/he's in!" Many of the pastors I have known (as many people in other vocations, too!) do not recognize their own shortcomings in communicating. I was hoping these two volumes might help bring about this recognition process and assist in developing more effective communicators in our pastoral leadership.

Again, as I stated in the Preface to Volume One, "These two small volumes are not meant to be primarily for skill development, a goal that can only be met satisfactorily through human interaction and practice in a classroom or workshop environment. Rather, these books have been written as a guide for readers to better understand what occurs when human beings (and particularly pastors) attempt to communicate. Hopefully, from this understanding will come a more effective use of those communication skills we already possess, and, coupled with the few new skills suggested here, each reader will enjoy a more fulfilling and successful ministry."

Chapter Ten
Informal Conversation

A Samaritan woman came to draw water, and Jesus said to her, "Give me a drink.". . . The Samaritan woman said to him, "How is it that you, a Jew, ask a drink of me, a woman of Samaria?". . . Jesus answered her, "If you knew the gift of God, and who it is that is saying to you, 'Give me a drink,' you would have asked him, and he would have given you living water." The woman said to him, "Sir, you have no bucket, and the well is deep. Where do you get that living water?" NRSV John 4:7-11

Now on that same day two of them were going to a village called Emmaus, about seven miles from Jerusalem, and talking with each other about all these things that had happened. While they were talking and discussing, Jesus himself came near and went with them. . .And he said to them, "What are you discussing with each other while you walk along? . . . Then beginning with Moses and all the prophets, he interpreted to them the things about himself in all the scriptures. . . (Later) they said to each other, "Were not our hearts burning within us while he was talking to us on the road?" NRSV Luke 24:13-15,17,27,32

Now there was an Ethiopian eunuch, (who) had come to Jerusalem to worship and was returning home; seated in his chariot, he was reading the prophet Isaiah. Then the Spirit said to Philip, "Go over to this chariot and join it." So Philip ran up to it and heard him reading the prophet Isaiah. He asked, "Do you understand what you are reading?" He replied, "How can I, unless someone guides me?" And he invited Philip to get in and sit beside him. . . He asked Philip, "About whom, may I ask you, does the prophet say this, about himself or about someone else?" Philip began to speak. . . NRSV Acts 8:27-31,34-35a

Certainly every informal conversation we have does not result in either conversion or a teaching opportunity. These three examples are chosen only to illustrate the existence of informal conversations in our Scriptures, and to show how these can be used for ministry when we are aware of the possibility.

The woman at the well was not drawing water in order to quench the thirst of her theological discussion club. She was not there to hear a sermon. She was at the well to draw water for her family, and she just happens upon Jesus who needs a drink. They converse as two human beings in an unstructured moment. But she probably was never the same afterward. An informal moment touched her in a way no formal sermon could. She might never have taken the opportunity to hear Jesus in any more formal setting.

In our walking and jogging culture, the example of the two men walking on the road to Emmaus and talking with a stranger should strike a familiar chord. Though these men appeared to be devout followers, it was the informal conversation that got their attention, not the synagogue teaching moment. Of course, with all the time many of us spend in our automobiles these days, the example of reading "on the road" and making efficient use of one's traveling time by discussing topics of importance is not far from our experience either.

Pastors meet such persons at the well every day, in the grocery store, in the cafe, in community organizations, on the street corner and on the road: people who might not be so receptive to a sermon on a Sunday morning. Please understand that I'm not advocating preaching to these people in their vulnerable and unsuspecting moments. I am advocating that we pastors be aware that God is present in these informal moments as in the more structured preaching opportunities. Even though we may teach this truth to our people, we do not always act as if we really believed it! I am advocating that, in the less formal moments of our lives, we offer ourselves to be channels through whom God's light can shine to others, that our informal conversations can be perceived as embodying God's Word as well as our messages from the pulpit. Each reader of these words can recall at least one such occasion in her/his own experience where this has been so. Our conversational partners have been touched by God's light without so-called, stereotypical "God-talk." Through this relational communication someone has experienced the presence of God in an atmosphere of acceptance and confirmation which we have encouraged and in which we have participated.

Characteristics of Conversation

Not all of us are completely satisfied with our conversational skills. Some of us are better at them than others. Each of us can improve. However, improving rests on knowing how conversations flow. Before we can gain additional skill (and it is a skill!) in conversing, we need to understand some of the elements in conversation.

As a starter, we need a brief review (from Volume One) of the general fundamentals of communication existent in informal conversation. First, we cannot not communicate! Simply being in a conversation, we are communicating something to the other person(s). Both our verbal and our nonverbal participation communicate messages. The other persons perceive messages whether or not we intentionally send them. We cannot not communicate!

What we say and how we say it in a conversation defines relationships. As stated in Chapter Seven, conversations can be viewed as having at least four different levels, each one defining a different relationship between the conversants. There's phatic which constitutes the "Hello, how are you?" social greasing that indicates the least trusting of the four levels, not necessarily shallow interaction, but rather an initial level on which each succeeding level builds, and a level many conversations never leave. The next level is gossip, talking about other persons in either a positive or negative manner. Conversing on this level indicates some trusting, in that the speaker is talking about people about whom the other conversant has some opinion, too. This

3

opens the conversation to agreeing or disagreeing with whatever impression and/or relationship the other person has with the subject. Some trust is necessary when doing this. The third level is labeled idea exchange, talking about specific non-person subjects on which some thinking has taken place. Here, because our ideas are psychologically understood as part of our being, a substantial amount of trust is necessary in the relationship. We don't easily open our mental processes for scrutiny. It takes a fair amount of trust to do so. The final level of relationship is called shared feelings. This level is divided into two sublevels, the first being shared feelings about concerns and people outside the immediate conversational relationship. Feelings are considered so very personal that we don't share them except with people we highly trust. Then the second sublevel, and the one that takes the very highest trust, is shared feelings about the person with whom one is conversing. When we converse on this level, we are taking the greatest risk, and consequently don't do this except with people we trust most. After all, the other person may not reciprocate those feelings, and we become very vulnerable. Yes, our conversations define our relationships.

Communication in informal conversation, and in any situation, is irreversible and unrepeatable. Once said, we cannot undo it. In conversation, unlike typing on a computer, we cannot simply hit the undo key. Time has elapsed, and what was said has caused a reaction on the part of the other person, and that will forever be part of this relationship experience. How those words will affect the relationship, of course, varies greatly. (I've always wondered how a jury can be directed to ignore any statement made by a witness or an attorney. The statement has been made; it is part of the jury's experience. That it must not be considered in the decisionmaking process is one thing, but to ignore it as if it never happened is impossible!) Not only can we not go back in a conversation, we cannot repeat the same words in exactly the same way to have the same effect. Time has elapsed. There was a reaction to the first time that became part of the relationship experience that was not present when uttered initially. Communication truly is irreversible and unrepeatable.

Communication is also contextual, equally true in informal conversation as in any other situation. There's the psychological context, the moods, attitudes, perception of status, perception of friendliness, etc., which affect how we relate to each other. Then there's the social context, that which is beyond perception, closer to the actual: our roles, power, social "rules," behavioral standards, etc. Next is the physical context, primarily the location in which the conversation takes place. It makes a difference in what is said and how it is said; e.g., in a library, a church sanctuary, the hallway, a cafe, the police station, as a whisper in close quarters, as a loud voice competing with a cheering crowd, etc. Fourth, there's the cultural context: traditions, customs, taboos, etc., which, though we are seldom aware of them, are always present in our relationships. Lastly is the temporal context. Time does make a difference, whether the conversation occurs late at night, early in the morning, in springtime or autumn, on Sunday morning after church services, during the weekday, etc. All of these five contexts interact with each other, and will affect any informal conversation in which we participate. To "test this out," the reader might think back to any conversation during the past week. How did the time of day affect it? the place you met? the role you played at that time? the perception of power? your mood? how you felt physically? your attitude toward the other person or the subject? By doing this, you will experience an awareness of context in your everyday conversations.

It might be worth looking at a few other observations of informal conversations that communication scholars have made. An interaction is considered to be a conversation when the "turns" are less than 45 seconds each; anything more than that is perceived by the participants as a "speech." A pastor can easily fall into the "speechmaking or sermonic mode" in the use of conversational time, and we need to be aware of its everpresent possibility. With the deference our laypeople often give us, whether we deserve it or not, they tend not to interrupt us as frequently as they would others, and we ramble on and on, turning a conversation into a speech.

Being "too articulate," a nice way of labeling a "smooth talker," will turn an informal conversation into a more formal situation, at least in the perception of many another participant. This is particularly so in some regions of the country where there is a mindset against the stereotypical smooth-talking city-slicker. Smooth talkers are often perceived as people who have carefully prepared for the interaction and know what they're going to say beforehand. True informal conversations are full of "nonfluencies," that is, expressions peppered with "audible thinking," with pauses to consider what the next word or phrase will be and how to utter it. Since we pastors have often been trained to speak well, we can be tempted to display this training, to the dismay of others, in our informal conversations. Such a display does not encourage the creation of an environment conducive to ministry.

Informal conversations involve fewer words, a reduced vocabulary. Using clergy jargon, or graduate school concepts, only impresses other clergy or graduate students. Our parishoners wish us to use those "highfalutin" words (e.g. "hermaneutics") only in our teaching or preaching moments, if at all. Conversational vocabulary is sparse, in whatever language we speak, limited to commonly used words and idiomatic expressions. If we wish to be included in conversations with our people, we need to remember this.

The last researched observation I'll mention here has to do with the rate of speech one employs in conversation. The rate at which a person speaks sends a commonly perceived message to others: the more rapid, the more formal and competent the speaker seems; the more halting (up to a point!), the more trustworthy the speaker is perceived. (Too slow and competency is questioned.) It seems that the pastor who deviates from the accepted regional rate of conversational speech will have some real problems to overcome in relating informally to the people of the parish. Many pastors who have moved from one region of the country to another (or from urban to rural and vice versa) have experienced this.

Toward a Working Definition

It's about time I offered a working definition of what I am calling "informal conversation." I agree with Goss and O'Hair that conversation is a "cooperative participation in managing dialogue." From that simple definition we can make a few observations. In Goss and O'Hair's words, there is "an implicit grammar for conversations that gives coherence to interaction." In other words, the conversation needs to make sense to the participants. It needs to be informative, truthful, clear, and relevant.

Conversation needs to be informative. This does not necessarily mean information completely new to the listener. Conversants are more than news-bringers. The information may concern something the listener has never heard before, or it may be only what the speaker thinks about the subject uttered in a manner the listener has not previously heard. Each is informative. If the words are the same from one interaction to another, and they are uttered in relatively the same manner, the listener will soon become bored or distracted. We need new information in our conversations, or old information told with a different slant. When a pastor visits an older person in an advanced stage of senility or Alzheimer's disease, s/he sometimes experiences hearing the same thing over and over again, told in relatively the same manner. We need to work hard in such a conversation. As someone else in a conversation with us must work hard when we tell the same story over and over again, or describe something they already know about in a way that is not new to them.

A conversation must be truthful, or be perceived as truthful, or at least the listener must perceive that the speaker believes what is being said is the truth. (We will discuss this tricky phenomenon when we discuss "ethics" in a later chapter.) Imagine a culture in which the truth is not expected, where everyone believes everyone else is not telling the truth. It would be chaos. Our culture is based on truth; we become very upset, angry, and eventually very cynical when we do not expect the truth from someone. We can follow the line of thinking and the flow of conversation much better when the narrower band of truth is expressed than if a conversationalist interjects an untruth from the universe of untruths available. To make sense, conversation must contain the perception of truth.

A conversation must be clear, or at least include opportunities to clear up what is mystifying. "Clear" here means that some understanding of what the speaker is saying is taking place. Informal conversations that continue will not leave the participants wondering what was really said. Sometimes our words and our nonverbal behavior do not match, and this results in more than normal misunderstanding when there is insufficient feedback, that is, limited opportunities for the listener to sort out what is really being communicated. To make sense, a conversation must be clear.

Finally, a conversation, to make sense, must be relevant. This may be its most important element. Contributions must be perceived as having something to do with the topic being discussed, or at least the theme or purpose of the interaction. The exception to this, of course, is tagging onto the last thing the other person has said, whether or not it relates to the original theme or topic. However, this is usually perceived as being relevant, too, whether or not it takes the conversation in another direction. It is relevant to the last statement made. In many informal conversations, and some very enjoyable ones at that, this latter exception is the norm. The theme of a pastoral visit may be to encourage greater involvement in the work of the church, but during the conversation other topics might be discussed, such as hockey, the theatre, canning, child rearing, etc. because one tag line followed another, not unlike playing a game of "Association." Sometimes it is very difficult to find one's way back to the original theme or purpose. The conversation has been enjoyable partly because it has been relevant, even though you haven't stuck to the original subject. Contrast this to an interaction (I cannot call it a conversation) in which every contribution is neither tied to the main purpose of the coming together nor to the last statement made by each person. There would be nothing to tie the "conversation" together, nothing coherent, although some statements made might be informative, perceived as the truth, and clearly verbalized. If the interaction is not perceived as relevant, it won't really make sense.

"Rules" of Conversation

Conversants employ numerous cultural rules to their interactions, most of which we are not aware; we just obey them because we've been taught to do so. Probably the most obvious rule is that we take turns speaking and listening. When one person is finished with a turn, s/he gives off signals (with voice or eyes or tilt of the head or with some hand gesture) that it is the other person's turn. When a listener wants to take a turn (e.g., in a three way conversation), there are signals, too: taking a deep breath, sounding an "uh" or "ah," using a hand gesture, or just plain interrupting. Sometimes a participant will ask a question at the end of one or more statements, indicating it's another person's turn to speak. In fact, every conversation seems to be constructed of these statement-response units. It may be question/answer ("Where's my concordance?" "It's on the file cabinet where you put it."), or inform/acknowledge ("Did you know that the story of Jesus and the woman at the well is only recorded in John's Gospel?" "Yes, I remember reading that somewhere."), or assertion/agreement ("I think the writer of John's Gospel must have had some other source for all those episodes in Jesus' life not found in the first three Gospels." "I agree, but since it supposedly was written many years later, it probably was from some remembered oral tradition."), or request/comply ("If you have any books on John's Gospel in your personal library, could I borrow them?" "Sure, but you'll probably find some more up-to-date ones in the seminary library.").

In an average conversation, most of these "turns" amount to only a sentence or two. Once in awhile conversants allow an extended-turn, a time of elaborating on some point or with a narrative or illustrative account of some experience. Too many details in the narrative, though, tend to tire the listener. These narratives need to be relevant, reasonably organized, and interesting enough to hold attention, else they will be perceived as an attempt to control the conversation or to satisfy a psychological need to be in the spotlight. There are people, and the clergy is not lacking in them, who enjoy hearing themselves talk so much that they frequently try for these extended turns in any way they can, from the less intrusive joke-telling to the more obnoxious long-winded dissertations. They have their reward, and it is usually avoidance if at all possible.

In conversation, as in all relationships, the element of "control" is a factor. Extended turns are sometimes taken by a conversant, but only quietly tolerated by the less assertive listener. Informal conversations that are mutually enjoyable will exhibit some semblance of equality. Many conversations are not renewed at a later date simply because one or both of the partners did not feel each had had an equal contribution in the former interaction. Pastors do have a lot to say, but if in an informal conversation they exhibit this control behavior, and do not allow for some sense of equal participation, they might find their next conversation with that person less than desirable. (The reader is referred to the discussion of Defensiveness in Volume One.) Each pastor should consider seriously the appropriateness of extended turns in their conversations, and limit these contributions to other situations in which their "long-windedness" is more likely to be tolerated.

I will not say much about "forced conversations," for they usually occur in an atmosphere charged with power-plays. This will be discussed in a later chapter. Suffice it to say here that when perceived power enters the picture, no matter how much one or more of the participants label an interaction as just an informal conversation, a whole new set of rules seem to apply: extended turns are "expected," and cooperative participation in managing the dialogue is greatly limited. A secretary who has betrayed confidentiality rules and who is being "set straight" by the pastor probably would not feel an equal part of the conversation; nor would the pastor allow complete equality in managing the dialogue. There is a power structure here, whether we like to admit or not.

The Role of Silence and Other Nonverbals

The presence of silence in a conversation is a tricky subject to discuss. Some people are far more comfortable with silence that others. In each conversation there seems to be an invisible line between acceptable silence and awkward silence. Sometimes silence is interpreted as a signal to end the conversation; sometimes it is perceived, especially when talking with someone with intense eye contact, as a ploy to get the other person to self-disclose. There are all kinds of possible interpretations. Most people, especially those who are sensitive to nonverbal behavior, seem to instinctively know where that invisible line is between acceptable and awkward silence. We can make only vague generalizations about this phenomenon: that silences will occur; and silent moments, like extended turns, should not be too long—the "too" part of this depends on the relationship, the location, and the occasion.

As implied above, an enjoyable informal conversation will exhibit sensitivity to nonverbal behavior, both the other person's and one's own. Especially in an informal conversation a person's "guard" is often down. We are more relaxed than in some formal setting. When this "guard" is lowered, we converse somewhat differently. We often become more animated. We don't always "think through" our statements before we make them. We are more spontaneous. Along with this spontaneity comes a perceived freedom to display nonverbal support for our statements or, strangely enough, a nonverbal denial of them which often sends conflicting messages. We pastors can train ourselves to look for these "signs," and be ready to assign meaning to them and to check what we have perceived for accuracy. As to being sensitive to our own nonverbal messages, awareness is the first step. As we become aware of what nonverbal signals we give, we then, more consciously, will try to make them less confusing. How do we discover what signals we give off to others in our informal conversations? By trial and error. By asking some highly trusted friends. By working with others in communication workshop or seminar settings.

Interruptions and Insults

A common behavior in informal conversations is the interruption. In the past, communication specialists joined well-known politeness experts in telling us "Never interrupt! It's not polite." However, in study after study since that advice was first formulated, we have discovered that some interruptions are very positive factors in conversational success. Interruptions of agreement serve the very positive function of encouragement and support for a point made ("Yeah. You're right. I agree wholeheartedly. I couldn't have said it better."). Even interruptions of disagreement serve a positive function. They enhance and focus the conversation, besides communicating to the speaker that we're listening and that we're interested in the interaction. Disagreement ("I can't accept that. I think you're wrong there. My experience doesn't support that.") can assist the coordinated management of meaning, which is what conversation is in the first place. A third kind of interruption is clarification ("I don't follow you. Can you go over that again? What do you mean by that statement?"). This, too, indicates interest and involvement. The last two types of interruption lean strongly towards being dysfunctional. The first is subject-changing. As we can imagine, this communicates either disinterest in the topic or a move to wrest control of the conversation from the one who currently "has the floor." ("Did you see that movie on television last night? I thought it was. . ." "I've misplaced my datebook. I'm lost without it.") The other dysfunctional type of interruption is making light of what the other person has just said ("I suppose that's OK, if you like that sort of morbid thing." "You know, when you just said that, all I could picture was Andy Rooney complaining about something on '60 Minutes.'") There are interruptions that have a positive effect, and there are interruptions that have a negative effect on a conversation. It is the wise pastor who knows the difference and employs them judiciously.

There exists in playful conversation something that is out of place in a more serious conversation. That is the insult. In some cultures and/or ethnic groups, the insult serves a very definite purpose, similar in effect to the "in-joke" as a verbal acknowledgment of a close relationship. The context and the players, whether they're in the "in" group or not, will determine if the insult will have a positive or a negative impact on the conversation. In the more playful conversations an insult will often be taken as a joke, as a friendly jibe, whereas in a more serious conversation the same insult might be taken as a "put down." With race being such a volatile issue in our country today, insults across racial lines are usually taken negatively. Within the same racial group, such an insult would be laughed away. Then there are some people who will only insult their friends, because to them insults are but another way of saying "I like you. You're my friend. We can be playful with one another." The context and the relationship are the determining factors as to whether or not to insult. If a pastor is of this personality type, of playfully insulting friends, s/he needs to be very sure of the relationship and very aware of who else is listening and who might be offended.

Being Assertive, Aggressive, or Submissive

A behavior that has received much press in recent years, and a topic that has experienced phenomenal growth as the subject of seminars and workshops, is "assertiveness." This subject found its current rebirth in the "feminist" movement in the last few decades. In discussing this topic, we focus on three hazily distinct categories called "submissive," "assertive," and "aggressive." Most people can distinguish submissiveness from the other two: allowing the other person to dominate the conversation and/or decisionmaking process. In a worship committee meeting, when there is discussion (mostly criticism) of the length of the Sunday morning services, the pastor who sits back and says little or nothing about the subject, for whatever reason, letting the other committee members make the decision to limit services to 45 minutes, even the occasional celebration of a high-holy-day, can be accused of exhibiting submissiveness (assuming the pastor has strong feelings about the liturgy!). We act submissive when we do not express our real feelings about a subject, or when we regularly inconvenience ourselves so we don't inconvenience the other person, or when we think ourselves less capable than the other on subjects dear to us, or when we behave in a manner that will keep attention away from ourselves, even momentarily. We often justify these behaviors by labeling them Christian virtues (self-sacrifice, humility, modesty, meekness, politeness, unpretentiousness, unworthiness). Only occasionally are these conversational models of Christian virtue. Sometimes this behavior is rooted in low self-image, as represented by the unspoken thought "I don't want to embarrass myself by revealing my inadequacies." Whatever we may call this behavior, and however we might justify it, one thing we do know: it is seldom conducive to honest discussion or conversation.

On the other end of the assertiveness continuum is "aggressiveness." This is attempting to impose our perception upon others, making decisions for the other, speaking in a manner that calls attention to ourselves, acting in an authoritarian way that takes power from another, speaking in a manner that runs roughshod over their feelings, using put-downs and manipulation as tools for maintaining a "superior" position. This description doesn't paint a very pretty picture, and it is difficult ever to justify it as pastoral behavior. However, such aggressive behavior is sometimes confused with being assertive. Acting with anger and exhibiting intense animosity has been perceived by some as "merely" expressing one's feelings, an attribute of assertiveness. I must disagree. We can express anger and intense frustration without being authoritatian, calling special attention to ourselves, or running roughshod over the other person's feelings. That is one of the main differences between being aggressive and being assertive.

What, then, is being assertive, and how do we do it? I like Richard Weaver's two word definition: "positive firmness." It, of course, is rooted in a positive self-image. "I am who I am; I have a valid perception, whether or not it matches yours or anyone elses; my feelings count just as much as yours, and yours as much as mine; we both have a responsibility in this conversation and I am accepting mine as I hope you will yours." With this attitude, a conversant will not cross that difficult-to-see line between assertiveness and aggressiveness. As I all too frequently told my students during my teaching years: "Share your perceptions as your perceptions, in full knowledge that if you don't say it, it will never be said, for you are unique and as an individual you see things a bit differently than any other person in the entire world. No one has experienced life in exactly the same way as you. We can all profit from your involvement in the discussion or conversation, as you can profit from ours." It seems to me, in any interchange of words and ideas, a person cannot go wrong in a conversation with this goal in mind. You will be operating within the bounds of conversational assertiveness.

Numerous communicologists have listed specific behaviors which indicate a person who is in an assertive mode. They have listed, among other behaviors: act strong and capable, be honest with your feelings without using them to manipulate the other person, don't overapologize, be willing to change your mind according to someone else's input, use "I" messages (because it is your perception that you are sharing), make honest requests of the other and be willing to accept their "no" as much as you wish them to accept your "no," don't be afraid to repeat an assertion that was either ignored, misunderstood, or simply not heard. All of these observations of assertiveness are helpful suggestions. However, I'm convinced that they are but behavioral elaborations of what I've shared with my students over the years, and what I have quoted above.

A Word About Starting a Conversation

Even though most pastors are probably above average on any sociability scale, and have some expertise in starting conversations with both strangers and acquaintances, and are fairly comfortable in doing so, there is always room for new insights and improvement. For example, consider the conversational categories observed by Alan Garner in *Conversationally Speaking*. He suggests there are always available three general strategies which can be chosen by a person wishing to start a conversation, plus three general topics about which such a conversation-starter can speak. The strategies are: ask a question; state a fact; or voice an opinion. The topics are: saying something about the immediate situation in which the conversationalists find themselves; making a comment on something about the other person; or making some reference to oneself. There are, then, nine possibilities for starting a conversation. Ask a question about the situation or about the other person or even about yourself. Voice an opinion about the situation or about the other person or even about yourself. State a fact about the situation or about the other person or even about yourself. My inclusion of the word "even" in the above sentences indicates my personal, and probably cultural, discomfort in beginning a conversation by focusing on myself when the other possibilities are open. However, I must admit to these possibilities and to my having used them once or twice. I offer Garner's insights both for those few of us who are uncomfortable, for whatever reason, in starting a conversation, and for those who might believe they need some honing of their already-held skills or could use another suggestion or two.

So What? . . .

Jesus with the woman at the well or with the men on the road to Emmaus, or Philip with the charioteer, as Scriptural incidents of informal conversation, do not by themselves demonstrate all the complexities inherent in such human interaction. But we can see in each, either obviously or by implication, many of the elements discussed in this chapter, from starting a conversation to cultural rules to extended turns to relevancy.

When we engage someone in conversation, one of the greatest of benefits is learning more about ourselves from the immediate feedback we receive. Of course, we not only learn about ourselves, but also about others, and about the world around us. When a pastor does her/his part in producing enjoyable dialogue, by understanding and applying the appropriate conventions of conversational interaction, all sorts of opportunities for ministry open. It may not be a woman at the well; it may not be walking along a Palestinian road; it may not be explaining the Scriptures while riding along in a horse-drawn vehicle. But modern opportunities abound: waiting for a bus on the street corner; standing in line to buy tickets; at the check-out counter of the grocery store; serving a meal to the homeless; sitting in the bleachers watching a son play football; between services at church. Too many to name. But they're there, believe me. And its a ministry we cannot afford to ignore.

Chapter Eleven
Interpersonal Relationships

(Deborah) sent and summoned Barak . . . and said to him, "The Lord, the God of Israel, commands you, 'Go, take position at Mount Tabor. . .Barak said to her, "If you will go with me, I will go; but if you will not go with me, I will not go." And she said, "I will surely go with you; nevertheless, the road on which you are going will not lead to your glory, for the Lord will sell Sisera into the hand of a woman." NRSV Judges 4:6-9

So (Naomi) said, "See, your sister-in-law has gone back to her people and to her gods; return after your sister-in-law." But Ruth said, "Do not press me to leave you or to turn back from following you! Where you go, I will go; Where you lodge, I will lodge; your people shall be my people, and your God my God. Where you die, I will die—there will I be buried. May the Lord do thus and so to me, and more as well, if even death parts me from you!" When Naomi saw that she was determined to go with her, she said no more to her. NRSV Ruth 1:15-18

When David had finished speaking to Saul, the soul of Jonathan was bound to the soul of David, and Jonathan loved him as his own soul. Saul took him that day and would not let him return to his father's house. Then Jonathan made a covenant with David, because he loved him as his own soul. NRSV I Samuel 18:1-3

Then Jeremiah called Baruch son of Neriah, and Baruch wrote on a scroll at Jeremiah's dictation all the words of the Lord that he had spoken to him. And Jeremiah ordered Baruch, saying, "I am prevented from entering the house of the Lord; so you go yourself, and on a fast day in the hearing of the people in the Lord's house you shall read the words of the Lord from the scroll that you have written at my dictation. . .Then they questionned Baruch, "Tell us now, how did you write all these words? Was it at his dictation?" Baruch answered them, "He dictated all these words to me, and I wrote them with ink on the scroll." Then the officials said to Baruch,

"Go and hide, you and Jeremiah, and let no one know where you are." NRSV Jeremiah 36:4-6,17-19

. . . we have decided unanimously to choose representatives and send them to you, along with our beloved Barnabas and Paul, who have risked their lives for the sake of our Lord Jesus Christ. . . After some days Paul said to Barnabas, "Come, let us return and visit the believers in every city where we proclaimed the word of the Lord and see how they are doing." Barnabas wanted to take with them John called Mark. But Paul decided not to take with them one who had deserted them in Pamphylia and had not accompanied them in the work. The disagreement became so sharp that they parted company; Barnabas took Mark with him and sailed away to Cyprus. But Paul chose Silas and set out, the believers commending him to the grace of the Lord.   NRSV Acts 15:25,26,36-40

Five examples of interpersonal relationships, chosen from among the many found in the Scriptures. Each different, yet with significant similarities, among them being: two people interacting through communication; relationships being influenced by context; the choosing of selective and appropriate strategies of interaction; evidence of consequences evolving from the choicemaking; acting and reacting based on individual perceptions; each relationship has a purpose and fulfills a need; each is more than a passing informal conversation and implies a background and experience with the other person out of which each speaks; all imply the probability of future interaction, and the very real possibility of pain if and when the relationship would experience severe stress or dissolution.

These Biblical associations are not untypical relationships. We pastors can identify similar relationships in our parishes: with someone who becomes a very close friend; with a person of special talent with whom we must work, although our styles of leadership might differ; with the church secretary; with a co-worker who decides out of her/his own integrity to part ways with us; with someone who "earns her/his own wings" after being emotionally dependent on us.

I should like to begin this chapter by agreeing with Aubrey Fisher, author of *Interpersonal Communication: Pragmatics of Human Relationships*, when he says that interpersonal communication and human relationships are really synonyms, that when we communicate with another person we are, in essence, relating to that person. So I have taken one word from each of these two-word labels and titled this chapter: Interpersonal Relationships. This best describes what I will be discussing in the following pages.

Jesus as the Model

Before I say anything else, I must affirm that I consider Jesus' teachings on "love" to be the model for all our relationships, his teachings by word and example. As I have come to understand the New Testament scriptures, Jesus' admonition, "Love one another as I have loved you," is the Christian prototype for all behavior. However, having said that, I realize such a statement is also vulnerable to a myriad of interpretations, as evidenced by the behavior of Christians worldwide. Even where this "loving" is understood as I perceive it, such an ideal remains just that: an ideal for which we strive. We so often "miss the mark."

This chapter stands firmly on that ideal: "Love one another as I have loved you." But it also incorporates what we have learned over the years as to how we might best achieve that ideal. I've tried to gather the most authoritive studies and up-to-date information and apply them to common pastoral relationships. This will be a discussion of the topic, not a cookbook of recipes (techniques) with which all the readers' relationships will suddenly and miraculously become satisfying. There are too many variables existent to make such a promise. Hopefully, through a better understanding of pastoral relationships in general, each reader will gain some insight which can be translated into behavior, thereby enhancing those relationships. I have studied communication too long to believe in any panacea.

21

Definitions of Relationship

To recap briefly: relationships are ongoing interactions, usually begun in informal conversation, but with a perceived (expected) future, however short or long that may be. This interaction (relationship) is longer lasting than are casual encounters; it exists (though possibly on and off) over a period of time, and in many cases is redefined numerous times during its existence.

Adler, Rosenfeld and Towne remind us that a relationship is not a "fraction" of the participants; that is, each individual owning part as an extension of being. Rather, a relationship is a "third self:" you, me, and us. It is a new creation. Fisher affirms that there are three "living beings" in a relationship: you, me, and the relationship (the quality of which is dependent on past experience and future expectation). Some judicial systems around the world, I am told, in divorce cases involve three attorneys: one for each person, and one for the relationship! The relationship is a living, breathing entity that needs as much representation as the other two.

Ingredients in a Healthy and Satisfying Relationship

Hybels and Weaver list two essential ingredients of good (satisfying) relationships, on which I have expanded and to which I have added. The first is commitment. There must be a perceived commitment on the part of both persons, an understanding that together they have created something new and will sustain, an appreciation of the present and an acknowledgment that this new creation will continue to live and be nurtured. A second essential ingredient is dialog, an understanding and application of Buber's "I and Thou" concept, that each person will interact with the other as a "thou" and not as an "it." This dialog would, of course, include substantial amounts of self-disclosure (Chapter Seven), of making oneself vulnerable by sharing the present with the other, what one is perceiving, what one is thinking, feeling, wanting, and doing. "Relational (reflective) listening" (Chapter Six) would also be part of this dialog.

Trust is also an essential ingredient in a satisfying relationship. Myers and Myers point out that hope and trust are separate behaviors, and I would add often blurred in the minds of pastors. Trust involves predicting that another's behavior will be consistent with past behavior, whereas hope may involve a desire for better behavior than has been experienced in the past. We can trust that someone will "stab us in the back" when that has been the pattern in the past; however, we can and do hope such a pattern will change for the better. A satisfying relationship will be low on defensiveness (Chapter Eight), and will be able to manage conflict (Chapter Nine) in such a way that results in more resolutions than increased tension.

One of the essential ingredients of a satisfying relationship is "time," an ingredient which often presents the most problem to a pastor. Relationships need time spent together in dialog if they are to be truly satisfying. Granted, a pastor cannot spend large amounts of time with each parishioner in order to meet the requirements of a satisfying relationship. And the larger the congregation, the greater this problem. It is impossible (some might even say unwise) to establish a close relationship with everyone in the parish. What is possible is to be perceived as accessible by everyone, or at least by most everyone. When a congregation perceives that the pastor's time is available to them whenever a need arises, the pastor has already solved this problem. When I know that my pastor will be with me in my hour of need, I have a satisfying relationship with her/him, regardless of how much or little time s/he has spent with me in less demanding situations.

This next ingredient of a satisfying relationship may not be absolutely essential, but since relationships do exist to meet our social needs, this is a highly important ingredient. I'm suggesting that others outside the immediate relationship acknowledge the association, that it is a friendship, that it is a pastoral function, that there exists some level of social/psychological/ emotional intimacy. This is not some secret liason or clandestine association; it is a publicly acknowledged relationship. This is a pastor and

Communicating: A Pastor's Job

parishioner; they are friends in Christ.

Many relationships, certainly not all, demand some behavioral flexibility, that the "rules" of the association can be redefined occasionally, depending on the outside demands and pressures one or both may perceive. This is the opposite of being "stiffnecked," as our scriptures sometimes state, applying the adjective to those who will not modify their behavior or attitudes for any reason whatsoever, no matter how pressing the human need. The pastor, in one of many possible examples, who will never respond to an interpersonal or spiritual emergency during time set aside for preparing the Sunday sermon, probably will not be perceived as a willing-relator. Such stiffnecked behavior sends a definite message to the people of the parish, a message most of the pastors I know want to avoid.

Every relationship seems to discover or create its own peculiar rules of conversation, be it the freedom to tell certain kinds of stories, or the limitation of never being able to sprinkle a passionate sentence with some less-than-pristine language, or the necessity of always being "politically correct." Some relationships almost demand no seriousness whatsoever. Others may be just the opposite: no attempts at humor will be tolerated. A nonverbal "touch" may indicate interpersonal warmth in one relationship, but in another could not even be imagined. In some relationships, every disagreement must be cushioned with words that reinforce the worthwhileness of the relationship. In others, such cushioning would be perceived as absurd or the weakening of the stated position. One relationship might be open to shared feelings, while another might be limited to idea-exchange. With so very many relationships existing in a parish between pastor and individuals, it takes concentration to keep within the "established" rules.

What happens if the pastor "breaks the rules?" That, of course, depends upon the individual parishioner, and how many like-minded parishioners have experienced the same kind of "rule-breaking." An occasional misstep can evolve into a perceived pattern if experienced by enough people. Only the first few apologies will be understood as "authentic."

24

Fisher reminds us that being "too open" can actually do harm and that every relationship needs to establish boundaries across which, for the security of the relationship, neither will transgress. If this is true of anyone, I believe it must be particularly true for members of the pastoral clergy. "Image" is certainly not everything, but it is something, especially in contemporary American culture. Being a pastor often carries with it a certain ideal image in the mind of the parishioner, an image which can be badly damaged if the pastor carelessly reveals something which can destroy that image with just a few words. Better to "chip away" at an unrealistic image than to destroy it in one fell swoop. If one must be extremely open in order to "be oneself," such a person should look at the long-range benefits of the relationship and weigh them against any short-term personal satisfaction. We should also recognize that when one person is very open, the other person either feels pressured to be as open, or feels very guilty over not being willing to do so. In either case, the relationship suffers from excess tension.

Another ingredient of a healthy and satisfying relationship is to recognize how unwise it is to be "objective." Indeed, it may also be impossible; therefore, if held as a goal, it can only bring frustration. In our culture, where objectivity is classified as a virtue in our sciences, it is not necessarily a virtue in our relationships, especially in those in which we are personally involved. Being "objective" demands standing apart and viewing without bias, separating ourselves from that which we are analyzing. Even if it were possible, such behavior would not enrich a human relationship as it does not communicate warmth or caring. It does, however, often invite a defensive response, being viewed as unwelcome neutrality or superiority, or even an attempt at judgment.

In Volume One I warned the reader against being too eager to give advice. However, there may be times in a pastoral relationship when advice-giving cannot be avoided. If and when such a situation occurs, the pastor needs to be very aware of the problem of offering "formula answers."

To tell someone who is stressed to the point of breaking to "relax" really is not very helpful. That person knows that. S/he needs to know how it can be done and still be acceptable as a person. This doesn't mean that the pastor's suggestions will be taken and acted upon; they may be, or they may not be. I remember a woman who came to me as her pastor with such a burden. She reviewed for me all that she was doing in and for her family, her church, and her community. She was, indeed, trying to be a superwoman, and the church was definitely benefiting from all her energy. When I suggested she might consider giving up some of her church activities for awhile in order to meet more of the demands of her family (where she perceived most of the pressure coming from), she looked at me in disbelief. These were all important activities that she was doing, and how could I, as pastor, even suggest such a thing? As I recall, she didn't take my suggestion, but at least I gave her something specific to think about, and didn't only restate her goal. She needed some relief; she was asking for it. She needed to relax, but just saying that would not have been very helpful, as it would have been too much of a "formula answer."

The foregoing illustration leads into the final ingredient I'll suggest as part of a healthy and satisfying relationship: be willing to take risks. I'm looking at risk-taking as making oneself vulnerable to possible negative consequences in hopes of gaining a greater positive outcome. The higher the risk, the more possibility of those negative consequences and less chance of the positive ones. I am not suggesting people communicate in a way that guarantees a negative impact on their relationship. That would be either masochism or sadism. I am suggesting that we apply those appropriate skills, as mentioned throughout these chapters, which, though never guaranteed, will likely enhance the relationship. Yes, there is some risk involved (such as wounded pride, temporarily relinquished control, embarrassment, etc.), and one must always weigh that risk against the worth of the relationship. However, not to take the risk is to settle for an often uncomfortable and tension-ridden status-quo.

A Pot Pourri of Thoughts on Relationships

Having offered a working definition for relationships, and describing some of the ingredients in a healthy and satisfying relationship, I should now like to share a pot pourri of thoughts and observations on the subject. The first is that each individual cannot define a relationship by oneself. Again, a common sense observation; yet one which is not always understood and/or accepted. I think pastors are often among those who struggle most with this fact. We frequently see ourselves as "fixers," as part of a healing profession. When one of our relationships is moving in a negative direction, we tend to fall into the trap of "fixing" the relationship by ourselves, almost as if the other person can be manipulated into cooperating. That simply is not so. Beyond the ethical issue in manipulating another human being, we need to be aware that it really does "take two to tango." A relationship is between two human beings, which means it's a cooperative activity (but, of course, not always a pleasant one). It's something that must be defined together. Each person retains a separate perspective, unique perceptions, expectations, desires, personal needs, internal and external pressures, and time availability. Together the individuals need to mesh these peculiarities into that third entity we call a relationship. If it can be done initially and continues to be meshed, well and good; if it cannot be sustained, the relationship needs to be redefined. But both persons must have a part in the redefining, especially when they might have very different perceptions of the relationship.

A second observation has to do with the above mentioned word: expectation. Everyone brings to a relationship certain expectations, which, among other factors, serve to judge the worth of a relationship. The role of expectation can be especially felt during a change of pastors in a parish. In the minds of some, the new pastor should be similar to the former one; or just the opposite. S/he should be as good as or better than the former pastor in preaching, or as a counselor, or administrator, or . . . All kinds of expectations abound. And the new pastor brings expectations, too. These people should respond to my preaching as well as my former parishioners did; or better, since this is a college town. Because this is a larger church, I won't need to spend so much of my time on administration, because with all the expertise in the congregation, the laypeople will take on that responsibility. Some members of the congregation will expect to be as "buddy-buddy" with the new pastor as they were with the former one, and will be disappointed if that does not happen. Many a pastor views a new appointment as an opportunity to begin anew, a chance to not make the same mistakes as s/he did before, or to bring what worked well in Smithville and apply it to Jonesville. Our expectations serve as evaluators of our relationships.

Each relationship the pastor has during every day of the year will be defined by both participants and be subject in large degree to the expectations each person brings to it. Will it be an intimate one? Will it be an authoritarian one? Will it be a "professional" one? Are we to relate as close friends? It won't make any difference if my pastor is male or female; or will it? Is gender to be much of a factor? How about age differences? And no relationships are the same! Since the pastor will switch types and intensity of relating many times a day, it is no wonder there is a notable "burnout" factor in the ranks of the clergy!

Another observation comes from a desire of some pastors to "get close" to everyone in the parish. Sometimes this is rooted in an obsessive need to be universally liked; sometimes from some other psychological need or developed image. However, it is not possible to achieve such a goal. Establishing close relationships demands expenditure of time together, building on common experiences, dialoguing, mutual self-disclosing, and all those characteristics we have discussed in this and other chapters. Time does not allow this for a pastor in a church of more than a few members. Even if it were possible, I'm not at all sure it would be wise to try. Parishioners have varying needs and make varying demands. Some people, because of past experiences, are very uncomfortable with someone trying to "get close." As much as a pastor's family hears about the needs of others, they can become jealous of the excessive time spent on the job and away from them. And I'm convinced that pastors need time to be apart, to be "by themselves," for contemplation, for prayer. Such personal time is often carved into in an attempt to make the necessary time for developing a large number of close relationships.

Every relationship has its own costs and rewards. Our goal is usually to receive the most reward for the least cost. Most of the time we manage this process quite well; but once in awhile we make a very poor assessment and suffer for it. The cost then becomes more than the rewards. Many a pastor, in an earnest attempt to help someone, has had it all backfire. The attention may be seen as paternalistic, or as demeaning, or even as romantic! Suddenly the reward derived from "doing one's ministry" becomes a cost too high to pay. When this happens, the relationship will need to be redefined to a mutual satisfaction, or even terminated if redefining is not acceptable to both parties. To drive this cost-reward point home in some of my university classes, I would ask each student to choose the person in this classroom to whom they are most attracted, and with whom they would most like to start a romantic relationship if the opportunity ever arose and if they were certain there would be a positive response from that person. They were not to divulge the name or identity of that person, and not even look at her/him during this exercise. On a sheet of paper, to be shown to no one and destroyed when they left the classroom, they were to make two lists: one headed "Rewards" and the other headed "Costs." Underneath those headings they were to list what they would anticipate if the imagined liason would occur. Of course, many of the students wanted to do this "in their heads" rather than on paper; it's much easier to deny. However, when I said I would do the same thing and write my lists on the board after they finished, they cooperated willingly. The discussions which followed made the exercise well worthwhile. The students understood that every relationship has both rewards and costs, and that this is especially so with newly developing relationships, which for many and varied reasons, impact and affect our older established relationships. The wise pastor will recognize this phenomenon, and apply a conscious effort toward receiving more true and lasting rewards from her/his relationships while avoiding the unwanted costs.

I would not be honest with the reader if I didn't admit there are some relationships over which we have little control. Granted: the above paragraph focuses on relationships of choice. Pastors, like other people in service vocations, cannot always choose the people with whom we must work and live. What then? Pastors who enjoy being martyrs have no problem with this; they just keep piling on the costs. The rest of us must find ways to increase the rewards while enduring the costs. Some of us will try to do this within the problematic relationship; others will find sufficient rewards in other relationships to give a semblance of balance in order to stay sane. When a pastor experiences extreme tension with some parishioner or group within the church, s/he may spend more time with the family or special friends to seek some sort of balance between the rewards of the latter and the costs of the former. Of course, the tension (cost) must be addressed at some point; but when and where can be decided at a time most appropriate for reducing it.

Aubrey Fisher, in his *Interpersonal Communication: Pragmatics of Human Relationships*, describes a control and empathy pattern that exists in every relationship. One person will communicate with "control words" or "giving-over control words," and it is up to the other person to respond appropriately for a pleasant interchange and smooth relationship. Giffin and Patton (*Interpersonal Communication*), years earlier, graphically described the same pattern with their four quadrants of "domination and friendliness." Who will control the conversational direction and subsequent decisions (if there are any) and who will follow the lead, plus how friendly or empathetic will both be during this interchange, are questions addressed in every interaction. If the same person is always dominant (in control), and the other is always on the responding end, that says something about the relationship. If both are friendly (empathetic) or unfriendly (not empathetic), that, too, says something about the relationship. If both people are satisfied with the existing relationship, well and good. If not, something about it needs to be redefined, else the costs will overtake the rewards.

When we have a choice, we form relationships for many reasons, so say our social scientists: because of attractiveness, or similarity of characteristics, or to complement some more extreme characteristic in our personality, or because that person obviously likes us, or we can give to each other something that person needs or wants, or we desire to be in the company of someone who is competant at what s/he is doing, or we see each other every day, or we have shared some secrets. These are all motivations for forming a relationship—when we have a choice whether or not to do so. However, the pastor does not always have such a choice. When a parishioner seeks out the pastor, for whatever stated reason, the parishioner may be operating under one of those listed motivations, but the pastor enters the relationship because doing so is part of her/his ministry. This is not to say that the relationship will never develop into one of complementarity (one's weakness is another's strength), or reciprocity (we like whomever likes us), or exchange (mutual benefits), or competency (expressing an expertise which is appreciated by another). It certainly could; and often does develop in such a way.

Improving Relationships Through Communication

Just how do we go about improving our relationships, wherever they are on the continuum: costly, balanced, or rewarding? Certainly the reader will not be surprised that I suggest "through more effective communication." But what does that involve?

Fisher identifies "competency" as the goal of every person

who is serious about communicating with another human being on a consistent basis. For him, relationship competency "involves a number of different dimensions, ranging from having a repertoire of behaviours to choosing appropriate relationship partners and even to deciding which relationships to continue and which to terminate." (*Pragmatics of Human Communication*) He defines "competency" itself as a judgment perceived by another. In other words, applied to the concerns of this book, a major goal of every pastor is to be a competent communicator in the eyes of the laity. But how is this done? And can it be controlled by the pastor? Of course not, since one person cannot control another's perceptions of anything, only contribute to the data on which other people build their perceptions. Pastors, through their behavior, can and do provide some of this data on which the laity will construct their perceptions of communication competency.

In addition to the many interpersonal skills I've described in Volume One, other suggestions have been made by numerous scholars, only a few of which will be mentioned here. Among the behaviors which will heighten this perception of competency, Fisher offers: avoid generalizing from one interpersonal relationship to another; develop and practice a wide variety of relationship strategies; don't confuse the emotions of the individuals at any given moment with the state of the relationship; know the rules of this particular relationship as they have developed and follow them; conversely, be a relational gambler, a participant who is willing to take some chances to better the relationship, rather than let it stagnate; accept as normal the existence of some tension and spend time and energy managing it; don't over-analyze either the relationship or the amount of satisfaction derived from it. In his skepticism with "being open," noted occasionally in his writing, Fisher labels such "openness" as a myth that needs to be identified and controlled. He advises, "By not being open in ultrasensitive areas, particularly those in which one of the partners is vulnerable and could be hurt, the communicators actually enhance their relationship and keep the quality of interaction high." In spite of this well-taken advice, a pastor should not be wary of self-disclosing as part of a satisfying relationship—only sensible in its application. (For further discussion on this very important point, please refer to Chapter Seven.)

Besides reiterating many of the more common suggestions as to what can be done to improve relationships, other communication authors add their own special experience and perception. Goss and O'Hair (*Communicating in Interpersonal Relationships*) remind us always to keep in mind that no relationship is static, that all are in the process of developing and evolving. Effective ministering demands that we remember this. Since individuals change constantly in response to both internal and external stimuli, the relationship they have with one another will also change. Each new interaction will affect in some way, however minute, the overall relationship. We cannot return to some point in time and erase some behavior or word expressed as if it never occurred. To forgive is one thing; to permantly erase a word or action from one's memory is asking for the impossible. The only option is to go forward and deal with feelings and perceptions as they have changed because of those events.

Adler, Rosenfeld & Towne (*Interplay*, 5th ed.) stress the importance of dealing directly with relational issues. In talking with other pastors, this is so difficult to do that they often avoid doing so. And this is very human! It is generally perceived as too painful. "How do you feel about our relationship?" is a very threatening question. As is, "Would you be more comfortable talking with another pastor?" Or, "Do you feel uncomfortable when we meet?" However, to dance around the topic by dropping hints or by "sending a John Alden" to check out a response seldom meets the need and often only complicates the situation by adding yet another perception to the relationship. Only on rare occasions is direct action in dealing with relational issues not advisable.

Adler, Rosenfeld and Towne also remind us of the importance of "face-saving" in our relationships. This is especially so in public. We often talk about the need for politicians to "save-face," but repress the thought that our fellow clergy or our parishioners also have such a need. Most people are concerned about their reputation; that is, how they are perceived in the eyes and minds of others. Relationships are not preserved intact when one of the individuals diminishes the reputation of the other person in the eyes of a third person or the public as a whole. Reputation influences self-esteem; therefore, saving-face communication strategies will also affect one's self-esteem.

Hopper and Whitehead (*Communication Concepts and Skills*), among others, recommend that we reevaluate our relationships from time to time. This can be partially accomplished in the privacy of our own thoughts, but more fully and probably more effectively in discussion with the other(s) in the relationship. Pastors are often forced, by the denomination's or local church organization's rules or customs, to reevaluate on an annual basis. However, such annual reporting is usually limited to statistics and somewhat vague statements in response to some overly generalized questions. More than this is necessary to be truly beneficial to any relationship, private or public. And, yes, such times of reevaluation do pose a threat to self-image and to the continuance of the relationship. But not to reevaluate has its downside, too: the possibility of stagnation; hidden feelings being intensified; acting-out on someone's part; tension from unrecognized or mystifying behavior. It seems to me, in comparing the possible costs to the relationship, periodic reevaluation is far and away the better choice.

Relationship Deterioration and Reconciliation

No one that I know likes to talk about the demise of a relationship. When a relationship comes to an end, there is a real sense of loss, a time when it becomes painfully obvious to those involved that a separate entity that they have created together is no more—in a real sense, a death has occurred.

On the subject of relational deterioration, Joseph DeVito

(*The Interpersonal Communication Book*, 4th ed) has drawn together and summarized much of the work of Murray Davis (*Intimate Relations*) and Steve Duck (*Dissolving Personal Relationships*). These authors, as well as others, have identified two kinds of relational death. The first is labeled "passing away," which is a gradual deterioration. The second is "sudden death," whenever an immediate dissolution occurs.

Let's look at the second kind first: "sudden death." In a marriage this might be an act of adultery, or physical abuse, when the relationship is suddenly and irrevocably broken in the perception of one or both of the partners. In the pastorate, a sudden death might be an act of broken trust, some kind of very inappropriate behavior, or even "getting too close to home" with some statement either in public or in private. The layperson may suddenly withdraw from the relationship, sometimes mystifying the pastor, but for a very valid reason in the mind of the layperson. I once knew a person who rather liked the new pastor and began enjoying the relationship, until it suddenly stopped and she would have nothing more to do with him. It was discovered later that the woman had heard that the pastor was married for the second time after having divorced the first. She didn't believe in divorce and held the pastor to a high moral standard which she felt he had betrayed. No longer was he valued in her mind as her pastor. A "sudden death."

Lest we pastors are tempted to condemn such "narrow-mindedness," we need to realize that we, being just as human, are sometimes so incensed at some comment by a parishioner that we make it obvious that we'd rather not relate to that person any longer. I remember an interchange with a couple in the aftermath of a devestating tornado, a conversation of which I am very ashamed. Their next door neighbor had been killed when her house came crashing down on her, but this couple had sustained only a scratch or two on their entire house. Such are the wiles of a tornado! As we stood on their lawn and looked at the pile of twisted timber next door, one of the couple said to me, "We didn't know we had lived such a good life to have God spare us, but the wicked are soon found out, aren't they?" Now my wife was in the hospital, in critical condition as a result of being blown out of our house by this same tornado. I remember clearly snapping back at this bewildered couple, "You expect me to believe that kind of theological rot with my wife wavering between life and death in the hospital?!!" I just spun around on my heel and left, being too tired and in no mood to discuss the theological implications of their statement. Needless to say, I didn't see that couple visit our church again. "Sudden death" of an infant relationship. I can only hope they found their spiritual needs satisfied in another congregation.

Probably the more common type of relational deterioration is the gradual one the scholars call "passing away." The causes of this kind of death are not so noticeable, until hindsight can occur. Looking back, we can see that possibly the attractiveness of the person or the situation had faded, or that the stimulation that once was evident had weakened, or that the former opportunities for self-knowledge and self-growth were no longer sufficient, or that the relationship was not reducing loneliness any longer—for whatever reason. Of course, much of the gradual change can be attributed to the unfulfilled expectations that began and developed in the relationship. Sometimes it may take only months or it may take many years for us to realize that our expectations are not being met anymore. This growing realization will be played out in many ways, psychologically, behaviorally, and emotionally, causing an unwanted stress which needs to be managed.

DeVito describes a number of behaviors which he has observed in deteriorating relationships, and which need managing during this slow dying process. Most of the behaviors he identifies in general relationships can be applied to pastoral situations as well. The people will begin withdrawing from contact with each other. They will not be in each other's company as often as in the past (not in church as much or seldom volunteering). They will not "make time" for each other. They will no longer "go out of their way" for the other person ("I'm just too busy."). Self-disclosure will decrease; since the trust level will probably go down, so will the statements which could make a person vulnerable be less frequent. Occasionally, the relators will make up reasons why they cannot be with the other person--a type of deception. Whereas at the beginning of the relationship each person focused on the other's good points or characteristics ("Our pastor gives excellent children's sermons!"), the focus slowly changes to an emphasis on the negative ("S/he spends more time with children than with the rest of us who pay the salary!"). The people will request fewer favors from each other, and what favors are requested will often be worded in a negative manner, or become devoid of emotion by assuring the other that this is simply an exchange, tit for tat, more of a "business deal" ("You baptize my grandchildren; I'll stay out of your hair."). Each individual will tend to blame the other for the strain they are experiencing, blaming them for one or more of the behaviors I've mentioned above, or even some kind of all-inclusive blame ("If we had a different pastor, this church would grow by leaps and bounds," or "My talents are being unused in such a stiffnecked congregation as this!").

What can be done to stop this deteriorating process, once it has started? DeVito suggests reversing the specific deteriorating behaviours. Stop withdrawing from each other's company, and force yourself to visit with the other person at every possible opportunity. Risk self-disclosing more; make yourself vulnerable (but I would add, be sensible about it!). Be supportive of the other person as much as you are able; avoid being too critical of the other person's behavior, and increase your positive evaluations. Observe social courtesies, both in public and in private. Ask favors of the other person; of course, favors they are able to do (don't "set them up" to say "no" to your request). Increase your complimenting behavior, including any nonverbals which can communicate "I care." For the pastor, I would add "Be available"—be willing to change your schedule if and when the other person calls with a real need. This doesn't mean altering important appointments on a regular basis whenever this person calls. It does mean occasionally "going out of your way" to be with that person, to say nonverbally "You are important to me."

Specifically targeting couples and others in affectionate relationships, DeVito suggests they participate in "cherishing behaviors." I think this can be applied to pastoral situations as well. DeVito describes these behaviors as being specific and positive, focused on the present and the future (not on the problems of the past), capable of being performed daily, and easily executed. I've seen pastoral relationships repaired by a "program" of sincerely given compliments both in public and in private, and by open acknowledgment that the other person's point of view is valid (even if disagreed with)—a program which fulfills all four criteria of "cherishing behaviors."

Goss and O'Hair refer to some reconciliation studies done by Krayer and O'Hair in which they interviewed numerous couples who reconciled after a deteriorated relationship. They identified ten reconciliation strategies that were attempted in these relationships: Martyr, Innocence, Realization, Persistence, Caring, Boastful, Denial, Apologetic, Directness, and Threat. Each of these strategies might also be illustrated in pastoral relationships.

In the pastoral setting, the Martyr might say something like "I know you're just trying to see how much I'll take and forgive before I give up altogether. I want you to know that I'll never give up and I'll always be a forgiving pastor." Innocence might sound like "If we can just sit down and talk about whatever it is that strains our relationship, I'm sure we'll find a way to smooth things over." The Realization strategy could take this form: "I've been spending too much time with constituents who'll never be part of our church and not enough time with faithful members like you." Persistence could sound like this: "You're the backbone of our church, and we need to have you active. My ministry is greatly weakened without it." Caring as a reconciliation strategy might sound like this: "I really care about you and your family. Is there anything I can do to show you how much I care?" The Boastful strategist might say "I accepted this pastorate because I and the committee thought my gifts and graces were the best suited to the needs and desires of this congregation." The pastor in Denial could express "Let's forget whatever problems we had in the past and start over fresh." Being Apologetic: "I'm sorry. Please accept my apology for whatever my part has been in putting a strain on our relationship." Directness might sound like this: "Let's try to work together again. The church can only benefit from our leadership and cooperation." Then there's always Threat as a strategy: "If attempts at reconciliation are just a waste of time, maybe both of us should look seriously at sharing our talents with another congregation."

I do not recommend any one of these "strategies" over another. None of them will guarantee success. They are but codified behaviors in a study of reconciliation. However, I do believe they are helpful in our discussion of reconciliation, not as recommendations, but as observable behaviors. Each pastoral relationship is unique unto itself, and what strategy will "work" in one will not necessarily work in another. Knowing what the possibilities are can enhance the choicemaking process and give the pastor a higher probability of success in the reconciling attempt.

Two more thoughts before I close this chapter. The first is that some relationships seem to develop a pattern of termination followed by reconciliation, followed by termination, followed by reconciliation, ad infinitum. Part of their relationship itself seems to be the redefining of their relationship. Individual relationships within the congregation may come and go, sometimes without identifiable reasons. This is to be expected, as frustrating as it might be.

The second thought is that, as difficult as it may be to acknowledge, especially for us pastors, some relationships will and do end. Death does occur: with our social selves, as with our physical selves. There simply is not enough present in the relationship to keep it alive, to keep it functioning. It dies. However, it is seldom completely forgotten. That relationship continues to work its effect on the participants. It becomes part of one's experience, and occasionally appears suddenly in memory to be dealt with.

Chapter Twelve
Working in Small Groups

Now when Job's three friends heard of all these troubles that had come upon him, each of them set out from his home. . . They met together to go and console and comfort him. . . They sat with him on the ground seven days and seven nights, and no one spoke a word to him, for they saw that his suffering was very great. NRSV Job 2:11,13

Without counsel, plans go wrong, but with many advisers they succeed. NRSV Proverbs 15:22

When the hour came, he took his place at the table, and the apostles with him. He said to them, "I have eagerly desired to eat this Passover with you before I suffer; . . . But see, the one who betrays me is with me, and his hand is on the table. . . Then they began to ask one another, which one of them it could be who would do this. A dispute also arose among them as to which one of them was to be regarded as the greatest. But he said to them, "The kings of the Gentiles lord it over them; and those in authority over them are called benefactors. But not so with you; rather the greatest among you must become like the youngest, and the leader like one who serves. NRSV Luke 22:14,15,21,23-26

Jesus went up the mountain and sat down there with his disciples. Now the Passover, the festival of the Jews, was near. When he looked up and saw a large crowd coming toward him, Jesus said to Philip, "Where are we to buy bread for these people to eat?" He said this to test him, for he himself knew what he was going to do. Philip answered him, "Six months' wages would not buy enough bread for each of them to get a little." One of his disciples, Andrew, Simon Peter's brother, said to him, "There is a boy here who has five barley loaves and two fish. But what are they among so many people?" Jesus said, "Make the people sit down." NRSV John 6:3-10a

Job and his three friends constituted a group. Proverbs speaks about a group of advisers. Jesus sat down at a meal with a group of his friends. Jesus and his disciples in the Gospel of John quotation formed a problem-solving group. Evidences of people working in small groups. A few people gathered for a purpose: to console, to advise, to fellowship, to solve a problem, or for any other purpose the participants desire.

Today we call them "committees," "task forces," "boards," "councils," "commissions," "panels," "cabinets." Whatever the label, they're basically small groups of people meeting together for a purpose. They are part of our world; for some of us, too large a part! But it's in our job description, and we can't get away from them. Sometimes, when the pastor is overwhelmed by small groups, Jean Paul Sartre's caustic comment in No Exit comes to mind: "Hell is other people!" Or Elbert Anderson's definition of a committee: "A thing which takes a week to do what one good man can do in an hour." Or Franklin Jones' bit of sarcasm: "An arrangement enabling one to share the blame with others."

I do not mean to imply that working in small groups is necessarily a chore and something to be avoided if at all possible. Some people may feel that way, while others feel just the opposite. Some pastors are very comfortable working in small groups, having discovered and nurtured the skills to make them an effective tool in ministry. In my conversations with pastors, small group work, especially in committees, seems to be one of the least enjoyable experiences in their ministry. Retired clergy frequently comment on how wonderful it feels to be free from the burden of committee work. Some of that relief certainly comes from their having free evenings, when most committees meet because of vocational schedules; but part of that relief also comes from the difficulty in trying to make decisions with groups of people and their divergent personalilties. This admitted discomfort in working with committees and other small groups is my justification for devoting an entire chapter to the subject, even though much of Volume One describes most of the interpersonal skills necessary to survive any small group experience.

Few seminaries emphasize small groups as opportunities for ministry. Committees are often perceived as necessary evils in the organizational church. To counteract this perception, some churches have adopted the practice of lighting a candle and placing it in the center of the group as a symbol of the Spirit of Christ. This helps each member of the group to be aware of God's Presence in their deliberations, thus taking the meeting out of the realm of "necessary evil" and putting it in its proper focus of "shared ministry."

Pastors participate in many different kinds of small groups, and during one's life-ministry will probably experience every kind. Groups today seem to be gathered according to purpose; that is, according to a specific deliberative reason for being. It may be for the expressed purpose of functioning as an integral part of the organizational structure, such as a committee or a task force (I'll be referring to this as a "problem-solving" group.). It may be for group counseling (e.g., pre-marital or parenting). A group might meet to give the members support for some common experience (e.g., elder-caregivers or rape victims). It might be to study (e.g., books of the Bible or denominational history). A group might meet to be trained under the leadership of some expert. Each of these types of groups share some common characteristics, as well as having some uniqueness. This chapter will focus on the commonalities, and rely on the reader to identify any uniqueness and apply the appropriate modification.

Some Common Characteristics of Small Groups

First and foremost, the basic characteristic of a small group is a shared goal, one that is acknowledged as common to all participating in the group interaction. This means that there is a difference between a "group" and a "grouping." The latter has no acknowledged common reason for interacting with each other. A grouping might be on the street corner waiting for the light to change, or in an elevator waiting to exit onto particular floors, or in a bleacher-section watching a baseball game. Each of these examples indicates the presence of people with individual immediate goals, who happen to be together, but have no reason to interact. They have no acknowledged tie to one another, other than being human beings in one geographical place attempting to accomplish their individual goals. (Unfortunately, sometimes we experience church committees that could be described similarly!) Therefore, this chapter will be discussing small groups as people with a shared goal interacting with one another.

What number of people constitutes a small group? Scholars who have studied small groups have settled on three to thirteen participants as being the parameters. One person communicating with oneself is labeled "intrapersonal" communication. Two persons interacting is called "interpersonal" communication. Therefore, three persons constitutes the low end of a small group. But what is the number at the upper end? These same scholars have arbitrarily set thirteen as the most participants who can work together effectively in a small group setting. Any more than that and the interaction opportunities become so minimal it becomes a public speaking event with multiple speakers. What is the ideal size of a small group? Five people. Why? Because at five the number of interactions is at the optimal level, as is the number of perspectives; that is, less than five and the variety of perspectives suffers, whereas with more than five the number of opportunities for verbal participation suffers.

Another way to look at the effectiveness of a small group, with special attention to the numbers involved, is to consider the number of relationships that must be sustained in the group, how size geometrically influences relational complexity. With two people, we have one relationship to consider. When another person is added, making three, we have three relationships to consider. Then when a fourth is added, we suddenly have six relationships in the group. Then add another person, totalling five people, and the number of relationships increases to ten, all needing attention in an effectively communicating group. Imagine adding another, to six this time, and the small group is faced with fifteen relationships in its midst. What about a group at the upper end of "smallness:" thirteen? The group would become a body of seventy-eight relationships! All going on simultaneously! (The formula for this number-game is number of participants multiplied by number-minus-one, divided by two.) As can be readily seen, adding people to the size of a committee can create problems for the participants as they interact with each other and as they attempt to communicate their thoughts and feelings in such a complex situation.

All groups must meet some place and the location of their interaction often influences their communication. There will be a difference in atmosphere between the pastor's office and the church's fellowship hall, as there will be a difference between meeting early in the morning at a downtown coffee shop and meeting in the parsonage living room over coffee. Meeting in a closed basement room is not the same as meeting in a bright and airy garden room—and the interaction among the group members will not be the same. Our surroundings do influence our behavior, no doubt about it, even to the color of the walls and the amount of noise that filters into the room. Human beings are affected by what they see and hear, as well as by their physical comfort level and the number of distractions they experience. It is a wise pastor who considers location important when scheduling a meeting.

An often overlooked aspect in small group work is the seating arrangement. There will be a difference in participation when the group is seated around a rectangular table and when it is seated at a round table. (There is real folk-wisdom in the label: "round table discussion.") Nonverbal messages are both sent and received by the positioning of the chairs in a group meeting, as well as by who sits in those arranged chairs. Equality is the dominant message at a round table; authority (or hierarchy) dominates the rectangle when the chair at one end is occupied by the one who called the meeting, or by the titular head of the organization (in the church it is usually the pastor). Elimination of the table altogether removes a psychological barrier from the group's interaction. Participants will then either feel more free to openly share, or more threatened and vulnerable (depending on the group's purpose, norms and cohesiveness). Studies have shown that proximity to the perceived leader of the group communicates status, and consequently heightens the participation of those so located. The further away from the perceived leader, the less participation occurs. The exception to this is the person seated directly opposite the perceived leader, a person who is most easily seen and who benefits from direct eye contact. Such a person will more likely be drawn into the conversation, sometimes even psychologically encouraged to disagree. I once served a church in which my primary antagonist always took a seat opposite me in any committee meeting we had, nonverbally communicating a very clear message. Short of assigning seats in every committee meeting (not a very practical goal), a pastor can only be aware of the communicative influence of seating arrangements and do everything in her/his power to decrease the negative effects.

Another characteristic of small groups comes under the heading of "group norms." These are the expected and informal behaviors of the group members. Disagreement is the norm in some groups; whereas in another group one would never think of raising a disagreement. In one group it might be expected that polite turn-taking occur; whereas in another group the norm is to "jump into the conversation whenever one can" regardless of whose "turn" it is. One group might prefer informality in dress and body positioning; another group might look askance at anything less than suit & tie and ramrod posture. Ethnic jokes might be acceptable in one group, whereas in another it would not. Is the pastor or another staff member referred to by first names, or by titles? As they meet over time, groups develop their own norms of acceptable behavior, usually by the trial and error method: if a new behavior is not rejected or negatively judged by anyone in the group, and it is repeated by one or more of the group, it then becomes a norm—an accepted behavior within the group. Understanding this dynamic of small groups is essential for any pastor who wants to be perceived as one of the community. What are the norms, and what price will I pay for not abiding by them?

Then there are the group rules, the formal, structured, and/or ritualistic guidelines in place to give some semblance of order. Does the group follow Roberts' Rules of Order? Does the meeting always begin with prayer? Do we handle "money matters" first? Is there a specific seat for chairing the committee, if indeed the group operates with a designated chair? Do participants refer to each other as Mr. or Ms. or Sir or Rev. or Brother or Sister or Friend or My Esteemed Colleague? Though these titles could be categorized as norms, more often than not such titles become operating rules, formalized and ritualistic ways to behave. Norms tend to be fluid, being altered bit by bit when the group collectively accepts different behavior. Rules are more static, having been formalized by the group. Occasionally breaking a norm can be interpreted as inadvertant behavior. Breaking an established rule is often interpreted more harshly, as being a rebel, as going against the group. The wise pastor knows the difference between norms and rules, and behaves accordingly.

The final general characteristic of small groups is their cohesiveness, or lack of it. This is the feeling of attraction members have for one another. How much do they enjoy being together, regardless of the stated reason for meeting? Do they chat amicably before the meeting formally begins? Are they interested in each other as people? Or are they completely task-oriented, having little interest in socializing? It should be no surprise to hear that there is a distinct correlation between task success and high cohesiveness. Beware of the group member who says, "Let's forget socializing and get down to business." That person does not understand the importance of cohesiveness for success. Of course, there is a danger of so much enjoyment in being together that the group never gets to the task. Too much conviviality can distract from the task at hand, be it solving a problem or learning a subject or supporting a person. An effective pastor will model a balance between cohesiveness and task, between caring for the people and getting the job done.

Why People Join Groups

Why do people join groups? Certainly because of shared interests or concerns or goals. But what do they get out of it, besides satisfaction in meeting those goals? I think it's important to look at the work of Schutz for some guidance here. As a practicing psychologist, Schutz identified three basic psychological needs people have which can be satisfied in group association: inclusion; control; affection. (These are similar to his categories of individual needs: fame; power; and love.) People join groups out of their need to be part of a community, to be included with like-minded people, to be identified with others in a cause, to overcome any sense of isolation they might otherwise experience. People join groups out of their need to control others, or to be controlled by them. A small group provides an atmosphere in which a person can practice control strategies and observe their effects. People join groups out of their need to be appreciated by others, to be loved by them, if you will, and to express in a safe way a need to share affection. Of course, these three needs are seldom in balance; they usually are felt in hierarchical order. Some group members might have a greater need to be loved, or to be included, or to control. One of the three needs might be very low in a person's need profile. Whatever these needs might be, and their importance in an individual's life, these needs will be expressed in the behavior of the person as s/he interacts in the group setting. The person with higher control needs will attempt to lead the discussion or set the direction of the group or manipulate others to a certain way of thinking or to keep the group on task. The person with higher affection or inclusion needs will tend to behave in maintenance roles, concentrating on keeping the group cohesive.

When I was in graduate school a number of years ago, one of my most frustrating experiences, yet also most rewarding and greatest learning experiences, was taking a course in Small Group Work from one of the leading researchers in the field, Ernest Bormann. Every student was assigned to more than one group with which to work during the quarter. One of my groups was going nowhere, being dysfunctional because of an unresolved leadership bid. It "came to a head" when one of our members flew out of our meeting one day and stormed into Dr. Bormann's office in tears, bewailing that the group wouldn't let her be the leader, and she was always the leader in whatever group she was in. I recall this scene only to illustrate an extreme need for control. She couldn't operate in a group in which she was not in control, so overpowering was that need in her life. On the other hand, there was another person in that same group who had extremely high affection needs, a person whom the others in the group wanted to be their leader. He refused, knowing that leaders tend to be more respected than loved; besides he had very low control needs. He wanted to function in a maintenance role, not a task role. He contributed to the dysfunctionality of the group because of his psychological profile. It would be profitable for a pastor to analyze her/his own psychological needs (according to Schutz's theory and categories) in order to better understand her/his group-role tendencies and the level of comfort or discomfort s/he might have in the roles assigned to her/him in working with small groups in the parish.

Roles in Small Groups

Schutz's theory applied to small groups leads nicely into the overall subject of group roles: what they are and how they are assigned. As stated above, roles are divided into two general headings: task and maintenance. Task roles are those that move the group toward its stated goal. Maintenance roles are those that attempt to maintain a comfortable level of sociability among the members of the group. The particular names given to each of these roles describes why these roles are placed in their particular category. Task roles include initiators, critics/analyzers, information seekers & givers, leader, recorder, lieutenant/assistant leader. Maintenance roles include encouragers, tension reliever, mediators, regulators, followers. Then there are negative roles that are sometimes assigned: withdrawers, resistors/blockers, self-focusers, rebel. These latter are counterproductive roles, to both task success and group cohesiveness, as their labels imply.

Each one of these mentioned roles has a purpose in small group life. None of the roles in the first two categories is any "better" than any other, although the role of leader is considered of higher status in our dominant North American culture, and thus is frequently the most contested role in the small group. Without the appropriate maintenance roles, the group would soon disintegrate as a social entity; enjoyment would drastically decrease; and the members would experience unrelieved tension. Without the appropriate task roles, the group would not move toward its goal; would not experience any great sense of accomplishment; and probably would not be very enthused about or capable of defending whatever conclusions they arrived at. Roles in both of these categories are necessary for a fully functioning small group. The above-mentioned negative roles are counterproductive, and in most cases are to be avoided, but dealt with carefully if and when they do occur.

I have mentioned a number of times that roles are assigned. What do I mean by that? According to Bormann's work with leaderless small groups at the University of Minnesota, members bid for roles during their interaction. He concluded that before a group meets, there is a role vacuum. During initial conversations in the group, members bid for roles with their statements and questions. If the group responds favorably to the bid, the member will attempt that behavior again and again, until the group "assigns" that role to her/him. If the group does not respond favorably to the bid, the member may try again, but upon receiving the same response, will soon back off, accepting the group's judgment that s/he is not to be assigned that role. This "bidding" and "assignation" continues until the major roles are all assigned. Occasionally a group will become dysfunctional because roles have not stabilized, especially the roles of leader and tension-reliever, the task and social leaders.

Let me illustrate. The group meets (without assigned roles at this point, even if it has an appointed chair or convenor) and begins to deliberate. Person A is the first to say, "Let's get started." This is a bid for leadership (a task role). Person B responds, "Not yet. Everyone is not ready." This is a challenge for leadership. If the group settles down and begins its task, Person A is temporarily (until it is reinforced) assigned that role, and the group looks to A for further direction. If the group continues to chat aimlessly, Person A's bid has not been accepted. There is usually a degree of tension at this moment. Person C cracks in a parental voice, "Has everyone gone potty? We're about to start." This is an attempt to break the perceived tension, a bid for the role of tension reliever, the social leader. If members laugh and relax a bit, Person C will have been reinforced in that role, and as time goes on the group will look to Person C to do the same thing next time tension is perceived. However, if no one laughs, or even scowls instead, Person C in all probability won't try to joke again to break the perceived tension. Person C might bid for some other role and see how the group responds; e.g., "Maybe waiting just five minutes would be OK," said with a smile and a nod to both A and B (a bid for the mediator role). The group's response will be either acceptance or rejection of that role. I admit that this is a very simple illustration of role assignation; however, it is not simplistic. Assigning roles is a very complex process involving everyone in the group, and who is assigned what role depends upon the personalities involved, their need-profiles, and their perceptions of self and others. These variables are conveyed through communication with all its dangers of misunderstanding. This is one reason some groups take so long in being stabilized, and why a few never get off the ground.

Not every role will be easy to identify. Some members will be assigned more than one role, depending upon the bids and the needs of the group. And members occasionally are allowed to switch roles. Every group is different, even though they have some common general characteristics. Church groups are no exception. Each study group, committee, task force, board will be different, even when comprised of the same people. Unlike what my fellow graduate student thought before her tearful outburst to the professor, we do not necessarily operate in the same roles in every one of our groups. Even the pastor will not be assigned the role of perceived leader every time. On the Board of Trustees, the pastor might be the information giver; on the Mission Board, the pastor might be the information seeker; on the Social Concerns Committee, the pastor might be assigned the role of mediator; on the Administrative Council, the pastor might become the leader; etc. If the pastor bids for leadership in every committee or group s/he serves on, it may be an indication of extreme status needs on the part of the pastor. If the pastor bids for the role of tension-reliever in most of the small group work in the church, that may indicate a rather high personal need to be loved. In either case, the pastor's contributions to the parish will be less than it could be, had the pastor been willing to acknowledge and to accept assignation from the group according to the needs of the group. Stepping "down" from leadership for the health of the group is sometimes the more effective ministry.

The Process of Group Development

Groups, particularly problem-solving groups, tend to move through a common process of development. Based on observational data from studies of small group development, communication researchers have created numerous models with which to understand this process. The one that makes most sense to me is the Fisher four-phase model, described clearly in his book, *Small Group*

Decisionmaking: Communication and the Group Process.
Pastors who tend to become impatient and/or frustrated in
working with small groups can benefit from understanding
this common process of group development. To realize that
what is happening (or not happening) in a group is common
to all groups and not because of a recalcitrant member or a
misapplied skill is extremely helpful in maintaining a healthy
emotional state.

Fisher's initial phase in small group development is called
"Orientation." When the group convenes for the first time
(or the first few times), no one wants to hurt anyone's
feelings, so they temper their comments with ambiguity and
tentativeness. As members of the group search for a
common attitudinal direction (what attitude is most
appropriate for the individual to communicate both toward
the other members of the group and regarding the content
of their interaction), they will "send up trial balloons to see
which way the wind is blowing." There will be an abundance
of agreement, although statements will remain rather vague,
general, and ambiguous. People are getting acquainted and
"feeling each other out."

Fisher's second phase is labeled the "Conflict" phase.
Ambiguity noticeably diminishes. Members begin to
articulate more clearly their attitudes and positions on
issues, many of which show through in candid expressions
of favor or disfavor. This is a time of testing ideas and
polarizing positions, a time of providing data and evidence
to justify perceptions and beliefs. This phase is often tied
closely to the struggle for leadership in the group. Members
"take sides." Personality conflicts sometimes become
evident, apart from positions on the task. There is far less
"beating around the bush." "How thoughts are expressed"
is often as important as "what thoughts are expressed," when
the communication vehicle becomes a point of contention,
whether that irritation is verbalized or not.

The third phase is the "Emergence" phase, and, according
to Fisher, probably the crucial stage in the development of
a small group. This is the time when there is a recurrence
of ambiguity, coupled with a softening of positions. Members

may not have switched sides; they just don't articulate their positions in as much of a polarized way. Fisher labels it "modified dissent." Mediating efforts abound. The group has become aware that it is a group, that sharp division will not accomplish the task. The members realize that they must "pull together," in spite of their differences. They are remembering that they established their attitudinal direction earlier (in the Orientation phase), so there is no need to search for direction. Now they must somehow apply their differences to their unified direction.

The final phase is labeled "Reinforcement." This is a time for actually moving toward consensus. Data is added to the discussion by all without regard for who held what position previously. Comments reflect a unity of opinion. Members reinforce each other, both socially and on task. The previous level of tension is no longer perceived. There is a sense of joy for having endured as a group, a pride in having accomplished something together. As one researcher so vividly described, in this phase "verbal backslapping" is very evident.

It should be obvious to anyone with even limited experience in working with small groups that these four phases do not last an equal amount of time. Groups move through these phases at their own pace. A particular group may spend an inordinate amount of time in sending up those trial balloons (Orientation) in an effort to avoid the disagreements that will occur in the Conflict phase. Another group might be polarized for hours in the Conflict phase, unable to modify dissent enough to move on because of personality conflicts or a struggle for leadership. Another group might experience so much softening of positions in the Emergence phase that it results in excessive ambiguity and its members are fooled into believing they have accomplished something, although they really cannot articulate what it is. Or the group might spend considerable time in reinforcement and congratulating itself for being so successful, that its time of celebration consumes as many hours as the other three phases put together. It seems to me that many church people are so afraid of conflict, thinking it "unChristian," that church groups oftimes attempt to bypass that phase altogether, and leap from Orientation to Reinforcement, from searching for a direction to "verbal backslapping" for having done such a great job. This leaves many people mystified as to what is going on, and encourages the perception that churches are either "doing nothing concrete" or being irrelevant as to the issues of the day.

A Few Words About Problem Solving Discussions

Most of the committee work within the church can be categorized as "problem solving discussions," that is, the participants have specific decisions to make that will probably be acted upon. They have a problem to solve, whether it is how to cut the budget, or how to deal with church school overcrowding, or what approach to take in reaching more of the unchurched, or how to improve the music program, or what to require of the new church secretary, or any of a myriad of issues that arise in the management of a congregation.

For years it has been assumed that if a committee will follow a certain strategy (e.g., Dewey's "Model of Reflective Thinking"), it will succeed in reaching its goal of decisionmaking with the least amount of stress and ambiguity. I do not doubt that taking such a prescriptive approach will do exactly that—and more. However, through my studies and in my experience of working with small groups, I have been persuaded that, as worthy as such perscriptive approaches are, and as helpful as they are in looking back to analyze what went wrong and what went right in the process, most groups do not approach decisionmaking in that way. Prescriptive models are excellent as analytical tools, but they are seldom followed in committee life. Individuals in a group simply do not interact according to plan. They test the waters, jump around from idea to implementation and from analysis back to testing the waters again. There really is no consistent pattern in small group decisionmaking. There are, however, certain procedures that can help a group move toward its goal, and when absent will hinder it from doing so.

One of these procedures is called "brainstorming." Whenever a solution to some problem is desired, if the group will attempt brainstorming (without deviating from its few requirements), a major step toward the solution will have been taken. Simply stated, brainstorming is the process of using the group members' imaginations by having everyone suggest all possible solutions (however practical or fanciful), but without evaluation from anyone (whether positive or negative) and giving all suggestions equal representation on a list available for all to see. Personally, I like to have listed at least twice as many suggested solutions as there are members in the group, more if possible. This kind of brainstorming serves to get juices flowing and everyone participating, plus so many suggestions that no one in the group will feel special ownership of any one idea, even one s/he might have included in her/his contributions. This is an exercise in leveling, setting the direction of democratic participation. After the listing has been exhausted, the group will then look at each suggestion as to its feasibility of solving the problem, not finishing this analysis until every suggestion has been given a fair hearing. When all the possible solutions have been discussed, the totally nonfeasible ones are weeded out, leaving only those with a possibility of meeting the criteria established.

This leads into a crucial aspect of small group decisionmaking: setting the criteria with which to evaluate each possible solution. Sometimes this is done before any brainstorming is attempted, and sometimes it can be done after the brainstorming session. But it must be done sometime! Else, a group can arrive at a solution that cannot be applied without major modification or even long-lasting damage to someone or something. If the group does not establish workable criteria by which to evaluate its decision (e.g., any decision must take into consideration denominational or ecclesiastical approval), and the committee decides on a particular plan or solution, later to discover that they should have taken something into consideration that they did not, further problems will ensue. People representing those criteria can get very upset and that can be troublesome. In the very least, it can cause the committee to "go back to the drawing boards." On the other hand, bungling this criteria-step has been known to split a church wide open! Setting the criteria by which the solution must be evaluated is extremely important to any decisionmaking body, and "in the trenches" of committee discussion, such a step must not be just assumed; it must be discussed and agreed upon.

The final ingredient I'll mention regarding the specifics of problem-solving discussions is the desirabililty—no, rather need—for scheduling some kind of followup after the solution has been implemented for awhile. It is very important to look at how the decision is actually working out, how successful it is and how satisfied those directly involved are. Without this kind of followup and subsequent feedback, many a "good" decision/solution has all too soon fallen apart. I do not believe a small group decision can be declared completed unless and until the "how, when & where" followup/feedback review meeting has been scheduled.

Some Concerns When Making Group Decisions

It must first be admitted that the basis of most, if not all, decisionmaking is not rationality. Group decisions, especially, are not rational, however much we would like them to be. Group decisions evolve from the interactions of participant members whose discussions evoke emotional responses based on their individual life experiences. These responses use the verbiage of rationality without being necessarily rational per se. In a real sense, we fool ourselves into believing we are something we are not. Advertisers have known this for a long time. The more successful commercials are aimed for the heart rather than the brain. Want to sell something? Picture a sweet little baby or a cute youngster in a confusingly-worded or ambiguous commercial and you'll still be successful. Why? Decisions are made with our emotions rather than with our intellectual powers. Should we expect anything different from a small group of people? The decision by a struggling young congregation to build a new church building when the pledging units are not sufficient in number to underwrite it is not a rational one, but an emotional decision resting on faith and hope. Likewise, a decision to continue ministering in the inner city, in spite of all the sociological data and rising crime rates which reason against it. Most of us highly educated people, whose intellectual powers have been honed by years of schooling, cringe when we are reminded of this human characteristic. Yet our own experience in working with people confirms this rather uncomfortable conclusion.

The problem of "group think" is another concern I have when discussing how people make cooperative decisions. "Groupthink" is the label given to decisions when the goal of completing the task as a unified group is more important than raising and discussing objections and disagreements. It is the temptation to gloss over differences of opinion in favor of unanimity, a temptation that was acted out with tragic consequences in the Challenger space mission incident, and a behavior that is especially tempting to church groups who have difficulty handling disagreement while trying to "love one another." When serving such congregations, pastors must teach the people that one can disagree without being disagreeable, that it's natural to have differing perceptions and even the honored Biblical personalities disagreed with each other from time to time, yet could indeed continue loving one another—that that which united them was far greater than that which divided them.

Another behavior to be aware of is called "risky shift" by Fisher. This is the strong tendency for a group to decide something together that they would not even consider deciding as individuals. It is the tendency as a group to think itself both infallible and invulnerable, perceptions individual members would not hold for themselves. There is something about the reinforcement of like-minded people in a group that permits occasional foolhardiness. Groups tend to gamble with higher stakes than individuals are wont to do. Groups tend to choose actions with a larger payoff, though with higher risk in attaining the payoff, than will individuals, who in their own private decisions tend to be more conservative. Members of a group develop a feeling of anonymity alongside the feeling of group support when making decisions, thereby lean towards making riskier decisions than individually they might do.

The pastor, in recognizing these three group communication concerns, will be less prone to be surprised when they become evident in a discussion. Without going into a complicated and confusing explanation about why these things are happening, the pastor, in seeing them coming, can more subtlely guide the group around these tendencies and help them achieve a more satisfying and lasting decision. These last two sentences provide a bridge to the next topic of leadership.

Becoming a More Effective Leader

The pastor, because of her/his high status position in the church and community, is almost without exception thrust into a leadership role, whether or not s/he has the necessary skills to function effectively in that role. For this reason alone, it is imperative all pastors understand this expectation and the major characteristics of leadership.

First, let's look at the three major styles of leadership: autocratic or authoritarian, democratic, and laissez-faire. Contrary to popular opinion, each of these three styles can be effective, depending on the group members and the situation. For example, as much as I personally might not recommend autocratic leadership in most situations, in the military it might well be the only effective style. This is the hierarchical approach, leadership from the top down, decisions being made by the one in authority and obeyed by the followers. Autocratic leadership may be the most effective style in groups that need to be motivated, that resist "getting started," or that have no direction and/or are not willing to decide on a direction. In such situations as these, the pastor may need to assume the leadership role, may need to "step into the leader-role vacuum," and expect the group to follow. In fact, the members may well be expecting this to happen. Certain denominations are structured in such a way as to invite this scenario to occur.

For a moment, let's look at what seems just the opposite of the autocratic style: the laissez-faire approach to leadership. For this style to be effective, the group must be composed of highly-motivated members who will respond to a laid-back discussion coordinator who trusts the group to achieve its goals with a minimum of guidance. Many pastors will find this style of leadership very difficult for two major reasons: one, having been thrust into autocratic and democratic leadership expectations for so long, it is sometimes full of anxiety and somewhat scary to take a "less-active" and less-controlling role; and two, discovering a group within the church who needs relatively little guidance might be so surprising that is just unnerves the pastor.

The third style of leadership is the democratic one, the style in which the leader (pastor, in this case) assumes the procedural leadership, actively guiding the group members toward its goal, whatever it is. This kind of leader truly believes the group can make a worthwhile decision, and makes sure all sides are heard, even helping a more reticent member articulate her/his point-of-view whether or not s/he as the leader agrees with that contribution to the discussion. A democratic leader will also be a good listener— to both verbal and non-verbal communication as it occurs among group members, and note both what is said and what is not said. A democratic leader will not enter the group environment with a hidden agenda (as an autocratic leader sometimes does), but will let her/his perceptions be known and be discussed as part of the whole process. A democratic leader keeps her/his responsibility clearly in mind, that although each individual member is important and needs to be heard and respected, it is the group and its task that must be the top priority. Of course, in the Church we're talking about the task of communicating the Faith as it has been transmitted to us down through the ages, and which is being acted out in the lives of the group members and the congregation. The pastor who forgets this has slipped into the laissez-faire style, whether it is appropriate or not, allowing the other group members full power to decide the group's fate.

We cannot leave this topic of leadership without reminding ourselves that the role of leader, as for example with the mediator and the tension-reliever, is given to the individual member by the group. Of course, there may be the appointed leader, who might convene the meeting or session on the basis of her/his title, official position in the organization, or designation by some authority outside the group. But such a person may or may not become the actual leader, who is assigned that role for other reasons that emerge from the needs of the group. How does one identify an "actual leader," apart from an "appointed leader?" This is accomplished by noting such behaviors as: to whom are most statements directed?; to whom do members look for confirmation of their statements?; who is allowed to make the more extended statements without being interrupted?; sometimes, who speaks most frequently?; who is expected to break long silences?; nonverbally, toward whom do most of the members orient their bodies? Two or more of these group behaviors will give an observor a rather clear idea as to who is really leading the discussion.

What does a pastor, who often assumes the role of appointed leader, do if and when someone else in the small group is given the role of actual leader by the group? This will depend on the perception of the pastor: Is the Holy Spirit speaking through this other person and the behavior of the other members? Is what is happening part of a power play by one or more members of the group? Will the group benefit more with this other person in a leadership position, rather than the pastor? Is the group just recognizing someone with more efficient and acceptable small group leadership skills? Can the pastor trust this other person to lead the group in the "right" direction? Or any number of other questions of perception. Beyond perception and ability is the question of self-image and self-esteem. Are the pastor's esteem needs so high s/he cannot let go of the leadership reins? Are these needs such that this "situational shift in actual leadership" won't create a crisis in leadership in other aspects of ministry?

These are real questions and concerns. One's answers and responses will determine one's behavior. Some answers will move the pastor as "appointed" leader to quickly and unobtrusively relinquish the reins and "follow" the perceived leader. Some answers will move the pastor to attempt strategies which will return actual leadership to her/him— strategies which might include speaking louder, quoting authority figures or fragments of Scripture, "wooing a lieutenant" (getting some other respected person in the group to agree or to resist or . . .). These describe the more recognizable strategies to regain leadership, but there are many others as well, both more subtle and more blatant, some of which could harm whatever level of cohesiveness might exist.

This last comment regarding cohesiveness is something the pastor must always keep in mind. There is a definite correlation between cohesiveness and productivity—up to a point. The more cohesive the group, the more the members like each other and like to work together, the more productive their deliberations are likely to be. When there are obvious personality conflicts or some amount of dis-ease within the group about the group or regarding the task, the deliberative result will be, more often than not, less than satisfactory. However, when the group likes to be together (cohesiveness) more than its members want to tackle the task at hand, productivity will diminish. Even though cohesiveness leads to task accomplishment, too much of it becomes counterproductive, and task-avoidance or procrastination is often the result. The pastor should be aware of this phenomenon and be prepared to help the group to walk that fine line.

Time, Conflict, and Patience

We cannot leave this chapter without mentioning three very important terms, one or more of which probably cause the majority of frustrations we have with small groups: time; conflict; patience. To assign the task of making a decision to a small group will usually take more time than to assign it to an individual. In our age of efficiency, and especially in many of our North American cultures, time is a valued commodity that must not be frittered away. Building relationships within a small group takes time. Hearing multiple perceptions on an issue takes time. The very process of small group decision-making takes time. Pastors always need to remember that the time spent in these small groups, with very few exceptions, is time well spent, both for the building of the Fellowship and the quality of the decisions made.

The second term is "conflict." As long as perceptual differences occur, we will have conflict. (Since Chapter Nine in Volume One discusses the subject of conflict in detail, I will not discuss it here.) Suffice it to say that many of us still try to avoid it, partly because we are taught to do so as children. Few of us are really convinced that conflict is a positive force in human relationships. Yet, discipline after discipline tells us that very truth. There can be no growth without conflict. In small groups, there can be no real and/ or lasting cohesion without conflict of some kind. We need to expect it rather than simply bemoan it. As frustrating as conflict is, it is a crucial element in small groups, so pastors need to expect it and learn how to handle it.

The third term is "patience." Most of us, pastors and laity alike, because we are so time-conscious and wish to avoid time-eating relationship-building or conflict management problems, become quite impatient with small group process. We think that there must be a quicker and easier way to do things than through a committee, and when we experience the complexity of the process, we frequently lose patience. Only when we are able to see small group work as important ministry will we get over this "patience-obstacle."

Maybe we wouldn't be going too far astray to reword that opening quotation from Proverbs: "Without decisionmaking small groups in the Church, plans often go wrong; but with many willing participants as advisors, they will succeed."

Chapter Thirteen
Public Speaking/Sermonizing

I am sending you to them, and you shall say to them, "Thus says the Lord God." Whether they hear or refuse to hear (for they are a rebellious house), they shall know that there has been a prophet among them." ... So I prophesied as I had been commanded; and as I prophesied, suddenly there was a noise, a rattling, and the bones came together, bone to its bone. Ezekial 2:4,5; 37:7 NRSV

Jesus told the crowds all these things in parables; without a parable he told them nothing." Matthew 13:34 NRSV

Peter, standing with the eleven, raised his voice and addressed them, "Men of Judea and all who live in Jerusalem, let this be known to you, and listen to what I say. Indeed, these are not drunk, as you suppose, for it is only nine o'clock in the morning. No, this is what was spoken through the prophet Joel: . . .Therefore let the entire house of Israel know with certainty that God has made him both Lord and Messiah, this Jesus whom you crucified." Acts 2:14-16,36 NRSV

Agrippa said to Paul, "You have permission to speak for yourself." Then Paul stretched out his hand and began to defend himself: "I consider myself fortunate that it is before you, King Agrippa, I am to make my defense today against all the accusations of the Jews, because you are especially familiar with all the customs and controversies of the Jews; therefore I beg of you to listen to me patiently. . . After that, King Agrippa, I was not disobedient to the heavenly vision, but declared first to those in Damascus, then in Jerusalem and throughout the countryside of Judea, and also to the Gentiles, that they should repent and turn to God and do deeds consistent with repentance." Acts 26:1-3,19,20 NRSV

A visit to any religious or denominational bookstore quickly reveals a plethora of books on preaching. There are so many helpful books on the market, written by competent authorities who offer suggestions to the pastor on how to preach effectively, that much of what I could write here would be only redundant. However, in this chapter I would like to highlight some of those suggestions, plus add a few observations and experiences of my own, both as a public speaker/giver of sermons and as a professional listener to speeches and homilies.

As the scriptural passages printed above indicate, there are many different opportunities for speaking publicly as a religious professional and a number of styles with which to accomplish those responsibilities. There is the "Thus saith the Lord!" approach of Ezekial and other Old Testament prophets. There is the parable approach of Jesus. There is the proclamation and indictment approach Simon Peter used in Acts 2. There is the defense approach employed by Paul before King Agrippa. And there are numerous other situational and stylistic approaches to public speaking recorded in our Scriptures, far too many for me to analyze or even to list. Instead, again, I will only attempt to highlight a few long-known behaviors and long-taught skills that lead to speaker success, and write about them from my own perspective as a lifelong listener and longtime practitioner of public speaking. I hope my observations, suggestions, and illustrative experiences will prove valuable to the reader.

Since sermonizing (preaching, from writing to delivery) is categorized under public speaking, I will be discussing the broader subject with reference to the more focused pastoral activity we call "preaching." That is to say, there are many occasions on which a pastor is asked to speak, but none more regularly than preaching a sermon. For this reason, the bulk of my comments will be on those aspects of public speaking that also apply to sermonizing.

Choosing the Topic

The first task is choosing a topic. For the lectionary preacher this is usually not difficult, inasmuch as the particular lectionary being used guides the pastor in her/his choice. However, there is usually room for a particular emphasis, and opportunity to make direct application to the local congregation. This is not the place to argue the merits and/or demerits of lectionary preaching. Suffice it to say that pastors position themselves on both sides of the lectionary/topical argument. If a lectionary is not used, the pastor must discover and choose topics suitable for that particular congregation. In either case, the bottom-line is knowing one's audience, whether it's through a systematic visitation program or through some other method of becoming acquainted.

This might be a logical place to insert a long-held concern of mine having to do with the pastor's preaching responsibility. We have been led to approach sermonizing with the sentiment: "What can I say to them next Sunday (or Saturday, or Wednesday)?" "What can I tell them?" As if the only vehicle of communicating the Gospel in a service of worship is the spoken word in the form of the traditional sermon of one person (the preacher) speaking from the pulpit and many people (the congregation) silently listening from the pews. It seems to me that a preferable approach might be "What do they need to experience?" and "How best can I facilitate that?" This opens the door to many avenues of communication, from dramatic scenes to impersonating a historical or Biblical character, from music to audio-visuals, from dialog speaking to small group discussions—even to a combination of approaches. Then the focus is not on "what I need to say," but on "what needs to be communicated." Making this suggestion is meant in no way to deprecate the importance of traditional preaching, only to admit that at times traditional preaching is not necessarily the best choice of communication-vehicle, but is often chosen because it takes less work and time (a reason that really deprecates sermonizing!).

If the occasion is other than what is normally called preaching in a scheduled service of worship, the pastor likewise must consider the audience and the occasion in the choosing of a topic. If the pastor is not given a specific topic on which to speak, somehow s/he must come up with something that will appeal to that particular audience. But how is this done?

When I was teaching public speaking in the university, I would assign each student the responsibility of listing at least fifteen subjects on which s/he could speak, if only briefly. Fifteen subjects which would be of interest to the speaker first of all. This took more time and energy for some students than for others. Then from this list they were to star those they would like to hear someone else speak on. From this starred list they would pick one subject which, with a good speaker, would not "turn off" the audience. That, then, would be their initial topic for a speech in and to the class. I would suggest a similar procedure for anyone, including a pastor who's been asked to speak on some occasion other than a regular service of worship, of course with the added suggestion that the topic be pertinent to the specific occasion and audience.

Identifying the Purpose

Once the topic has been chosen, there are other things that need to be addressed. The first is "What is my purpose? Is it to inform? Or to persuade? Or to commemorate?" The answer to this question will determine how the speech will be most effectively organized. It will also determine what illustrations or examples are chosen—and what forms of "proof" are needed. The specific purpose (inform? persuade? commemorate?) may impact on the use or non-use of audio-visuals. Will the approach stimulate the audience's emotions or will only their minds be targeted? These and other questions cry out to be answered when we, as speakers, ask "What is my purpose?"

When this question is asked of the preacher, more than one answer, of course, may well be given—a response that tends to "muddy up the waters;" whereas the single purpose speech is more focused. The preacher in today's American culture cannot count on all members of the congregation being at the same level of understanding or commitment. The sermon must be informative; that is, some members simply do not have the Biblical or ecclesiastical background necessary to understand even the most basic tenets of the Faith. Then there are those who have nearly the equivalent of a seminary education! And there are many people, probably most people, at numerous points in between those two extremes. The sermon must be sufficiently informative to meet the needs of all the listeners, in itself a daunting challenge!

In addition, the sermon must be persuasive. The preacher must attempt to move congregational members from point A to point B; that is, from where they presently are in their spiritual and/or service life to where God wants them to be. To do this, some kind of persuasive organization of thoughts and ideas must be employed—along with an appropriate delivery. At the very least, the preacher tries to persuade the congregation that what is being said is important enough for them to listen!

Then, further, the sermon will be commemorative. It will call attention to the One in whose Name we speak. It will be a "remembering together" of the One who created us and who sustains us—and who loves us! The sermon devoid of this purpose will call into question the motives of the preacher!

So—what do we say about purpose in the construction and delivery of a sermon? Obviously, it will not be single-focused. However, to make all three purposes of equal focus would seem to me to be an impossible task, and overly frustrating to anyone who spends time and energy attempting it. Depending upon the current emphasis of the liturgical calendar, the situation in the local church, and the needs of the specific congregation—admittedly, determined by the pastor's perception, one of the three purposes will take on primary importance for any one sermon. However, when the first draft of the sermon is completed, it should be checked over as to its fulfilling not only it's primary purpose, but also it's two secondary purposes. Criteria for judgment will include the time spent on each, the emotional impact of each, and the memorability of the illustrations used.

Choosing the Content

Next, we come to the question of content. Once the primary purpose has been identified, what material do we gather and include in the public speech or sermon? Far be it from me to make specific suggestions regarding content! What information and material a speaker uses will be relevant to that speaking event only—to the speaker's motivation, purpose, theology, occasion, audience, time limits, setting, and to the speaker's level of communicative ability. This comment applies both to sermonizing and to public speaking in general. However, I would like to offer a couple generalized suggestions.

The first has to do with, admittedly, a pet peeve of mine: the temptation on the part of many public speakers to start a speech or sermon with a joke of some kind. I, and other listeners with whom I have shared this, wonder why some speakers insist on doing this. Is it an attempt to manipulate our response to the speech or speaker, to tittilate our attention and catch us off guard; in other words, to control us? Is it an attempt to reduce the nervousness of a speaker who perceives her/himself as incompetent? Is it a prophetic commentary proclaiming the dullness of the speech that is forthcoming, that it cannot stand by itself as an arresting presentation? Should I prepare myself for a light-hearted speech that will take little effort to understand and remember? Or is this a speaker who is attempting to emulate a stand-up comic, in which case I need to listen with other critical criteria in mind? These are the questions of a discerning audience, unless the joke or humorous story immediately ties in with the thoughts and words to come— and the more directly the better. This kind of opening for a speech or sermon must apply, in a manner obvious to the audience, to the rest of the message! Not to do so calls into question the motives of the speaker.

Having said this, I do suggest, however, that every speech or sermon have at least one illustration that will catch the attention of an audience. This may be in the form of a story, an example, a parable, a descriptive experience, or the like. In my years of being a listener to sermons and other kinds of speeches, as well as being a public speaker, I have noticed that audience members remember the illustrations much longer than they remember the more abstract idea. Sitting in the pew, I have noticed teenagers dozing off or otherwise not paying attention to the sermon, until the preacher starts a story or other illustration; then their posture noticeably changes to one of giving attention and showing active interest. When listening to speeches, especially sermons, we adults experience the very same changes: our minds tend to drift occasionally, and they are brought back to the subject at hand whenever the preacher starts offering an example or telling a story or making a point by sharing some experience, especially a personal one.

I do want to comment on the use of family experiences as illustrative material. Though this can be a very powerful way to get a point across to a congregation, many a "preacher's kid" has been hurt by this kind of public disclosure. As one who gave in to this temptation more often than I might have, I speak from experience. Three of my four children never seemed to be bothered by what Dad said about them from the pulpit, but the fourth child, being much more private and self-conscious, made it clear that she did not want to hear her name in any of Dad's sermons. I tried to do as she requested. My point here is that some children (and spouses) don't want their private and home life shared with the church family. And the preacher should abide by their wishes, especially as the children grow older and can react to their name or situation being discussed. Then there's another concern that has just recently been brought to my attention: self-conscious voyeurism on the part of some members of the congregation; that is, as one person shared with me after hearing a preacher relate a very personal family experience, "I felt as if I were peeking in their window and seeing things I had no right to see." It seems there is a very fine line between appropriate self-disclosure and inappropriate self-disclosure from the pulpit. A wise preacher will be aware of this possibility and very careful not to slip over the inappropriate side.

A third general suggestion I would make regarding content, especially in preparing for a sermon, is the reference and relationship to Biblical teachings. Some readers will question my even mentioning this point, assuming that every preacher will naturally do this. I mention it because every preacher does not naturally do this. Since we pastors are called to preach as part of our ministry, preaching, too, needs to be grounded in our commitment to the Faith—and our congregations need to hear this grounding, and to hear it regularly. The sermon in our weekly services of worship is still the most available means we have to share Biblical Truths with our people. Such sharing can be accomplished effectively with either Lectionary or Topical preaching; obviously it is more convenient to do using the Lectionary readings as the starting point for the message, but beginning with a Topic relevant to the congregation's perceived needs and searching the Scriptures for its perspective on the subject can also accomplish the same thing. In either case, we are proclaiming that the Scriptures are relevant to our world today.

The fourth and final suggestion has to do with the use of humor in sermons and other kinds of speeches. Exposure to Elton Trueblood's *The Humor of Christ* would immediately put a positive spin on this. Trueblood makes a very clear case for the effectiveness of humor in the sharing of the Good News. Since Jesus used humor so effectively, the door is open for us to do likewise; however, some of us are not as proficient at this as others of us are. We need to know our capabilities, and abide by our limitations, if indeed being humorous is one of them. William Shakespeare knew the power of humor as he occasionally inserted a bit of "comic relief" in his tragedies, giving his audiences an opportunity to relax before the next heavy and poignant conversation or interaction. Studying those plays as presentations of a theme and/or point of view, especially with an eye to his comic reliefs, can enhance a preacher's understanding of the use of humor in serious talks. Practice through trial and error, especially in "timing," and noting the response of the audience, is the only way to become comfortable in using this very helpful skill. Using humor in public speeches can be a very effective way of communicating an important message, but it is one of the most difficult skills to develop and hone—and it takes lots of practice.

Organizing the Speech/Sermon

A speech/sermon must be easy to follow! The audience/congregation should not be expected to put most of its listening energies into figuring out where the speaker is going. A clearly organized speech is the only way such clarity can be accomplished. An unorganized speech unnecessarily distracts an audience from the message and there can be no excuse for it.

A metaphor I like to remember when developing a speech is that of giving a present to the audience. The introduction and the conclusion are like two ends of a ribbon which encircle the body/present and tie it into a neat little package. In the conclusion, the speaker refers in some relevant manner to what has been said in the introduction, thereby "tying" the speech together. This is a very simple type of organization, one most of us learned in elementary school on how to write a composition: introduction, body, conclusion. At least the beginning and the ending are usually easy to follow. What the speaker does with the body is sometimes a real problem.

There exist a number of tried and true models of speech organization, only a few of which I will mention here. I don't want this chapter to duplicate what many readers have already learned in college or seminary. I do want to highlight models I believe are most effective, and to do so requires a brief review of them.

Of course, there's the age-old sermon organization

employed by some circuit riders (at least stories have come down to us that some used it): "You tells 'em what you're goin' to tell 'em; then you tell 'em; then you tell 'em what you told 'em!" Such organization might have worked well on some occasions by some preachers, but it has its limitations, particularly with the more "sophisticated" listeners of today.

Seminarians often joke about the "three point sermon," so much so that we often look for three points when we listen to someone preach—as if there were something magical about three points. Such behaviour might have its roots in the limits of memory; that is, more than three points are more difficult for a congregation to remember. Of course, there's the "theological" rationale, too, that's sometimes offered: it's a Trinitarian model!

Speeches/sermons that are categorized more as informative rather than persuasive have a number of possibilities as to how they might be organized. The speaker can choose whichever strategic order s/he thinks would best communicate the information: chronological (according to a time pattern such as 2000 BC, 1000 BC, 100 AD, 900 AD, Present); spatial (Israel, Europe, America); causal (this leads to that, if this then that); problem solution (existence and seriousness of a problem followed by a workable solution); topical (Methodism, Roman Catholicism, Judaism, Unitarian). The parts of each organizational model become as hooks to hang an audience's recollections of what has been said.

Speeches/sermons that are categorized more as persuasive rather than informative also have a number of possibilities as to how they might be organized. The inductive (reasoning from the specific to the general) organization might be employed, or the deductive (reasoning from the general to the specific) organization. Of course, both types of organization need supporting material for every step in the persuasive attempt. Each of the above-mentioned classical models might be accompanied by an escalating emphatic delivery or by a rational point by point delivery mode.

Of all the persuasive models I've seen, the one I prefer is an organizational pattern called "Monroe's Motivated Sequence." It is based on the psychology of persuasion, and was developed in the 1930's by Alan Monroe of Purdue University, and is often employed in radio and television advertising. The five steps in this more detailed model are labeled Attention, Need, Satisfaction, Visualization, Action. A stewardship talk or sermon could be developed without much problem using this model. Some startling statistic about American giving patterns, or reading a modern version of the Rich Young Man's encounter with Jesus, or even a brief dialog between the preacher and a layperson in the pew might serve as the Attention Step. An enumeration and description of the Needs of the Church (both local and denominational) would follow, plus the need of the individual to give. The way to meet these needs (Satisfaction) is by moving toward the goal of tithing ("If only half of the people in this congregation tithed, we'd more than double our budget. . ."). The next step (Visualization) is crucial to this model. It should be a word-picture of what would happen if the satisfaction step really occurred, and if possible a description of where it is currently working, such as in the Church of the Open Door in Babcock, Iowa, and to Philip Keane and his family who are members there. The final step (Action) consists of urging the congregation to do likewise and to reap the benefits of tithing. Each of the five steps should include supporting material; that is, evidence that the congregation will accept. Monroe's Motivated Sequence could act as the organizational pattern for many a talk or sermon, from prayer-life to social action, from loving one's neighbors to accepting forgiveness, from studying the Scriptures to attending worship more often. I do not mean to infer that this model can be used for every sermon or talk, nor should it be; I only highlight it to show the importance of organizing one's ideas and as a good example of how it can be done.

I want to say two more things before leaving this topic of organization. The first is that a speech/sermon needs only one conclusion! All too often, for my taste anyway, speakers do not stop speaking after an effective conclusion, but rather talk on and on with conclusion after conclusion. When the point has been made, the audience/congregation is ready to move on to the next activity in their lives, be it entering into open discussion, going home, the next part of the liturgy, or getting to church school class or to fellowship hour. And frequently the second and third "conclusions" are anti-climactic, and actually detract from the message. I offer a rule of thumb here: "When you've stated your best conclusion, the speech/sermon should be over. So sit down and/or get on with the next part of the program!"

My final point on organization is related to this conclusion-problem. It is the problem many speakers have with timing and the length of the speech/sermon. Whether we judge it to be fortunate or unfortunate, the fact is that most people in our modern American culture are programmed to pay attention in fifteen minute segments. This can be pushed another five or seven minutes, but not beyond without negative results. Of course, there are exceptions, as with a scheduled lecture or something like that. But for the most part, and especially in our mainline services of worship, fifteen to twenty-two minutes is about all we can expect of full attention to a monolog talk. Yes, in Puritan times clergy were booted out of their pulpits if they didn't speak for at least an hour, but times have changed. Yes, in some other cultures around the world, longer speeches are expected and revered, but not in this one. Whereas in other times and places the question was asked, "Wasn't your message important enough to spend at least an hour on it?", today our audiences advise, "If you can't say it in fifteen (or twenty) minutes, don't bother saying it!" Whether it's actually true or not, our people feel very pressed for time and let us know about it by their lack of attention or squirming—or, in some cases, by their absence.

Delivering the Speech/Sermon

Many a person in the pews was first attracted to a

particular local church by the obvious delivery skills of the preacher. In many cases, it seems that the more dynamic or charismatic the pastor/preacher, the more listeners to their speaking they'll acquire. However, the more discerning person in the pews will soon realize that, as important as these delivery skills are, they are not the whole story. When a listener praises a speech or sermon only for the speaker's delivery skills ("Isn't Rev. So & So a great preacher?!"), but remembers very little of the Message ("But I can't remember what s/he said."), the preacher has failed. Yes, delivery skills are important, but they must not detract from the Message. They should act as a faithful vehicle of the Word.

The one skill that seems to be most appreciated by an audience or congregation is the ability to communicate enthusiasm. When a speaker is excited about the subject and/or the opportunity to speak on this occasion and to this audience, most listeners will give that speaker an ear— at least as long as the words continue to justify that attention. It is truly unfortunate that some pastors act as if they have forgotten the root-meaning of enthusiasm: "en-theos;" that is, "in God," or "possessed by God." It seems to me that this is what we pastors are called to be, and we should communicate our appreciation for being so, particularly in our preaching, a public event which gives us the opportunity to express it. Let's not be afraid to communicate enthusiasm in our public speaking!

A Speaker's General Orientation

When we are delivering our speech or sermon, beneath whatever delivery skills we have and beneath the words themselves, is that basic orientation every speaker has—an orientation that can determine the very success or failure of the speech. "On what aspect of the speaking situation is my primary focus?" Am I oriented toward myself, most concerned that I come across as credible, as a good speaker? Am I most concerned with how I look, or with my voice tone, or with my skills or lack of skills as a speaker? Most children and young people, being emotionally self-conscious, and many beginning speakers, too, start here. Some experienced speakers never seem to leave this orientation, and their long-term satisfaction rate shows it. A second orientation or primary focus is on the audience. This seems to be the orientation of modern advertising: present whatever is pleasing to the audience. Analyze the listeners as to their needs and desires, and you will have a successful speech. This is very much a reactive approach to public speaking, in essence letting the audience determine the speaking event. The third orientation or primary focus some speakers exhibit is on the message. This is particularly tempting for both preachers and teachers. The Word is so important in our lives, whether it be in the Bible or in a textbook, that our primary orientation rests there. ("I'm not important; the audience is not really of most importance; only the Word, and all that Word means to us, is important. Our job is to drop the Message into the minds and hearts of the audience, and the Word will do the rest.") Some very successful evangelists seem to exhibit this orientation, and far be it from me to negatively criticize it. However, for the rank and file of us, I think there is a better way as we go about our pastoral duties and fulfill our preaching responsibilities. I label it the relationship orientation. It is an existential focus on the here and now, on what is being "created" in a particular place at a particular time and among the people present. I, as speaker, am important; you, as listeners, are important; the Message, certainly, is important. But what is happening between and amongst us right here is my primary focus. The question that's uppermost in my being as a speaker is "how can I best and most appropriately create and sustain a desireable relationship with the people before me?" (As I write these words, I am struck by the notion that this might be called "pastoral preaching.")

One of the main components of this "pastoral preaching" is listening to one's audience, in the sense of being aware of the feedback the congregation is constantly giving, interpreting it, and responding appropriately to it. Such preaching is "here-and-now" preaching. Lest the reader think this approach to speaking prohibits the speaker from preparing adequately in terms of the material to present, let me quickly say that is not the case. One can prepare for a speech/sermon in anticipation of the relationship that will be created between speaker and audience. ("My speaking these words to this audience at this time will create what relationship?—Will it be one of trust? or one of antagonism? or one of leader/follower? or mutual commemoration? or mutual respect? or hero worship of me? or parent/child? or what? And is this what I desire?"). Then, when the speech event actually takes place, the speaker will be in that relationship, and, reading the audience's feedback, will make the necessary adjustments if they are needed—always with the goal of sustaining a desireable relationship to that particular audience. In other words, preparing the sermon in anticipation of the relationship; then, if necessary, during the speaking, adjusting the speech to sustain the relationship—but always with an eye and ear to the relationship being created. All this takes careful listening!

I have always envied (confession!) African-American preachers speaking to African-American congregations. Unlike their counterparts in the European-American culture, these speakers are given audible feedback. They have a better handle on the relationship being created. Those "Amens" have a very real purpose in that they reflect the existing and/or emerging relationship, one which speaker and audience are building together. The preacher rooted in the European-American culture must read silent feedback, and that is always subject to misinterpretation. I recall one time many years ago when I was preaching and there was an older minister in the congregation, someone whom I deeply respected for his intellect and his spiritual insight. On one point where I was a bit shaky on the interpretation of a scriptural passage, I happened to look directly at him. He was scowling and shaking his head from side to side. Needless to say, I was concerned. After the service I asked him about that objection or disagreement. He denied having one. When I described his behavior at that one moment in the sermon, he had to think about it. Then his face lighted up as he remembered a little boy in the pew right in front of him who was making faces at him and trying to disrupt the service. My minister friend had scowled and shook his head at the little boy. We both chuckled at how easy it is to misinterpret silent feedback. If my sermon had not been written down in a rather tight organizational pattern at the time, I would have been tempted to respond in some way to that misinterpreted feedback at the moment it was given.

Manuscript, Notecards, Outline, Off-the-Cuff, or?...

This illustration raises the question of speech or sermon form. Is it better to speak from manuscript, speak extemporaneously (from note cards), or just off-the-cuff (approach the speech event with an idea or scriptural passage and start talking)? The answer depends on the personality and skills of the speaker, besides on her/his understanding of the preaching task. Just where does God's Spirit do its guiding and where is the speaker most likely to respond? in the study? in the pulpit? If in the pulpit, the preacher will probably tend to speak either off-the-cuff (impromptu) or extemporaneously. If in the study, the preacher will probably tend to speak from manuscript or extemporaneously.

Personally, I steer away from off-the-cuff speaking. I must admit to having done it on occasion, but I am not comfortable doing so—and I never remember just what I have said in the talk. My listeners have been kind in their praises when I have done so, but they have also reported my having made certain statements that I did not think I had made, and hadn't intended to make. Also, I have more "I wish I had remembered to say this or that" memories, which add to my discomfort. If one is going to do impromptu speaking, it is very helpful to have a stock organizational pattern in mind to provide hooks to hang thoughts and points on, such as the patterns described earlier in this chapter.

I started out my speaking/preaching ministry with extemporaneous speaking. I would do my prayer-preparation and research in my study, jot down ideas on paper, arrange them in some sort of organizational pattern, write them in outline form on 3 X 5 cards, and practice preaching from those notes. This worked quite well, with the only real problem being the length of the sermon. It seems that each run-through would prompt an additional illustration or a clarification of a point made—right up to and into the preaching event itself (a problem that besets an "associative" thinker more than a "logical" thinker!). A fifteen minute sermon would suddenly become thirty or thirty-five minutes! The sometimes necessary on-the-spot adjustments in the pulpit added even more time. Then there was a problem I had not anticipated. As with impromptu speaking, the audience/congregation members would occasionally comment on statements they "heard" but I didn't think I had said. And there was no available data to confirm either perception. (My sermons were seldom taped.)

Therefore I moved to "manuscript speaking" whenever possible—not because it was the better way to go, but because I was more comfortable with it, being who I am. And it helped me to overcome the problems I was having with public speaking, without diminishing the positive aspects of the speaking event itself. I found myself spending much more time in the study in preparation for any speaking occasion. Putting words down on paper (on the computer screen today) helped me to be more precise in the expression of my ideas and insights, reducing the misunderstanding that is always present. In both my praying and writing I could focus better on anticipating the relationship to be created between my audience and me. My organization was always "tighter;" that is, easier for an audience to follow. I would practice using the manuscript until I knew where each thought and word was on every page. When I got into the pulpit or before whatever audience I was to speak, I knew exactly what I was going to say, and I had fewer temptations to add an illustration or clarification. Not to say that I never added anything, only that I did it less often. With the more exact wording in front of me, I could concentrate more on establishing the eye contact with my congregation that is necessary for relationship-speaking. Because of this, I became more cognizant of their feedback, as silent as it often was. And, yes, occasionally I did add or subtract a thought or expression when I perceived from feedback a need to do so. Although the presence of the manuscript was never a secret, I was delighted to hear every once in awhile surprise in the voice of an audience member when s/he discovered that I was not just speaking from a few notes. And when someone "heard" something different from what I had said, I could usually rely on my manuscript to clear up the matter. Then there was that rare response of wanting a copy of the sermon to send it on to someone else. It was available—as preached.

Manuscript preaching is not for everyone. There are at least two related reasons why someone might not stick with it over the long haul. 1) In manuscript speaking, it is very easy to get locked into the words printed on the paper; after all, much time and energy have been invested in creating these particular words. To concentrate on our own "beautiful words" means that the relationship between speaker and audience will then take a back seat to the words on the page in front of you. 2) When the speaker excessively attends to the printed words by giving them the bulk of eye-contact time, the manuscript becomes a barrier between audience and speaker, communicating to the audience that the manuscript is more important than they are, thereby reducing any hope of a positive relationship being sustained. Until these "problems" can be overcome by internally focusing on the immediate relationship rather than on the words themselves, and by habitually sustaining effective eye contact with the audience, a speaker would do listeners a favor by staying away from manuscript speaking.

A POT POURRI OF THOUGHTS ON PUBLIC SPEAKING:

Non-verbals in the Speaking Event

Now is the time to mention the non-verbal

communication of a public speaker/preacher. I can only add to some of the content already covered in Chapter Three of the first volume, in which I discussed an overview of the subject and related it to a number of pastoral situations.

There seems to be a trend to more informally presented sermons in which the preacher comes out from behind the pulpit and walks around the chancel, sometimes even into the nave aisles themselves. This certainly does communicate a more informal atmosphere during this part of the service of worship. There are all sorts of arguments for and against this behavior. Having delivered sermons/homilies in both manners, my only reaction to this trend is that such informality depends upon the skills of the speaker, plus the goals and comfort level of both the preacher and the congregation. Any pastor who is thinking of going this route on a regular basis needs to consider carefully a number of factors. It is true that the pulpit does create somewhat of a "barrier" between speaker and listeners, and that, as pulpits are often elevated and built larger than they practically need to be, pulpits nonverbally communicate "status." However, on the positive side, "elevated" also means better sight-lines, and size (and elaborateness) can signify respect for the interpreted and spoken Word. Most congregations still place high credibility in what is communicated from the pulpit as it nonverbally reinforces the spoken Word. Although the "walking-around" sermon does reduce the problem of separateness between speaker and audience, it, too, has its problems. Many smaller churches (and some larger ones) have not invested in a highly effective all-purpose and adaptable public address system. They continue to be quite costly. Some members, therefore, cannot always hear the "wandering preacher," both because of a limited mike system and because of the human dependence on complementing their hearing with a continuous view of the speaker's mouth, which is often difficult to see. Then, too, especially when the preacher walks the aisle, the words s/he speaks can sometimes "come too close" and seem targeted at the person or persons nearest the speaker. Some people in the congregation, having been inculturated with certain distances being appropriate in certain situations, will react very defensively from the perception that "their space" has been invaded. Some preachers have been known to stop in the aisle and "chat" with someone in front of her/him, something that can communicate many and varied meanings. I have seen this done effectively, and I have seen this done when the result was deep embarrassment. Again, preaching in a roving manner needs to be considered very seriously before being put into practice—because of what it communicates nonverbally.

Another nonverbal behavior to be considered is eye contact, something I have mentioned previously in a number of contexts. Whether a preacher stands in the pulpit, or behind the Table/Altar, or at the lectern, or somewhere else in the chancel or aisle, s/he must maintain eye contact with someone in the congregation a majority of the time. This does not mean with a sweeping glance covering the congregation in general, a behavior which is often substituted for real eye contact which is "eyeball to eyeball." It has been said that the famous Jonathan Edwards, in his "Sinners in the Hands of an Angry God" sermon, droned through the entire text in a rather monotone voice and never looked up to establish eye contact with his audience; yet that sermon is reputed to be the cornerstone of the Great Awakening experienced in the American colonies in the early 1700's. He had his congregation shaking in their seats, a reaction that surely underscores the power of the Word when spoken to a very receptive audience; however, I sometimes wonder what the reaction would be if Edwards had looked intently at his audience when he uttered that message! Would they have changed their normal behavior when relating to the "heathen" Indian, for example? Would they have become less judgmental and more accepting of Christian diversity? I wonder. Occasionally I find myself listening to a speaker who either looks in my direction all the time or none of the time. When that happens, I wonder what the preacher has against the part of the congregation being ignored, or if s/he has a "crick" in the neck. That behavior is disconcerting, to say the least. Individuals in all sections of the congregation need to be included, or "eye-balled." Not to do so communicates a message the preacher may not have intended.

Distracting behaviors is another nonverbal problem some of us have. I remember a beloved seminary professor who had a very patterned "dance" when he preached: he would stand on one leg for a few moments, then stand on the other, back and forth while he spoke, the other leg crossing over the "working" leg. Some of us seminarians missed many of his insights, I'm sure, as we concentrated on his legs, counting the number of times the professor "danced." Other behaviors which can distract listeners might be "unneccessarily hitching up one's trousers;" or "stroking one's beard;" or moving one's hands and arms as if "directing a choir;" or "adjusting one's glasses;" or . . . A helpful suggestion which might identify possible distracting behaviors is to practice the speech or sermon in front of a full-length mirror—and be honest with what you see! I suggested this to one of my sons who was in a speaking contest during his high school days. He was very surprised at seeing his distracting movements, particularly his "choir directing" arm-waving. Without his identifying those distracting nonverbals, he might not have scored so high at the state level, even though his content and voice delivery were exceptional. A number of the college students in my public speaking classes had similar experiences with their full-length mirror rehearsing, and they admitted benefiting from it in spite of the temporary embarrassment they felt when a roommate would "catch" them practicing.

Using Visual Aids

In the past, preachers seem to have made minimal use of visual aids in their sermons, relying on the power of the spoken word alone. Occasionally one would use some small object to accompany a point being made, such as a cup of water or piece of rope or head covering or dollar bill or stone.

The exception, of course, has been the so-called "children's sermon," which has often been presented with the help of a visual aid. We have discovered that children learn better and faster when we use such aids, but we have been remiss in transfering this discovery to the teaching of adults. It's almost as if we have overlayed (out of context) Paul's admonition to the people of Corinth onto our preaching task: "When I became a man, I put away childish things." Yet, I have observed that a congregation of adults will pay strict attention to many children's sermons and then yawn their way through the regular sermon. An occasional and wisely used visual aid in a sermon can add lasting power to the spoken word. Among other benefits, if the visual aid is a common object, the message will be brought to mind whenever that object is seen outside the church setting. I once preached a series of sermons, during the summer months to a congregation of regular travelers, on road and traffic signs: "One Way;" "No U Turn;" "No Parking;" "Slow. Children at Play;" etc. Many individuals in that congregation reported remembering the sermon each time they saw those signs—and for a long time afterwards. I recently was privileged to hear a sermon by the pastor of the church to which our son belongs, in which this pastor effectively used a slide projector during the sermon. The slide shown was a shadow portrait of some person. In speaking about humans as being created in the "image of God," this preacher accompanied the slide with words similar to these: "This shadow that we see is not the whole person. We need to see the image of God beyond the shadow." The shadow portraits (silhouettes) given to us by our grandchildren, now hanging on our dining room wall, suddenly took on a whole new meaning for me! It is so very true that all of us seem to be more persuaded when we can see what is being said!

In teaching "secular" public speaking, we instructors always include the use of visual aids in our lesson plans—and for good reason. The "eye-gate" is very persuasive; of course, when reinforced by the "ear-gate." This is true whether our audiences are children or adults, whether they are expecting secular words or religious words. The principle and the benefits are the same. One caution I would give to a speaker, in or out of the pulpit, is to remember to speak to the audience and refer to the visual aid, not the other way around--that is, not to talk to the visual aid and only occasionally glance at the audience. As with manuscript speaking, audiences must continually be assured that they are more important than the visual aid, and that importance is communicated by regular and consistent eye contact. Another reminder I would give to the user of a visual aid: make it large enough so everyone in the audience can see it, and that goes especially for any print material being used. Few things frustrate an audience more than if a speaker is referring to a visual aid that cannot be seen.

The Public Address System

In our modern world of communication technology, we are often expected to use a microphone and public address system. This technology has made exercising our diaphrams unnecessary. When our normal conversational volume can be heard by hundreds of people in a congregation with the help of a mike, we have no need to project our voices. Or do we? Unfortunately, when we do not have a public address system or, like most technology from time to time, it is not functioning properly, we either are unable to compensate for it or just assume the people can hear us anyway. Such an assumption can result in our audiences not hearing all that we say, thereby opening the probability that excessive misunderstanding will occur, especially since audience members tend to "fill in" information from their own experiences (see Chapter Six) which leads them down entirely different paths than we are traveling. (There is some evidence that partial deafness is on the rise; consequently, we are seeing more and more people "filling in" words that they do not hear.) It is wise for preachers not to depend highly on their microphone systems, but develop a speaking voice that will carry their message without such reliance.

We must not leave the subject of microphones without a practical word about using them. Many a public speaker makes a couple of unfortunate assumptions. The first is that all microphones are the same. Nothing could be further from the truth. Some are mono-directional and some are multi-directional. There's a big difference in how they are used. Some are voice-activated, and some are not. (Many a speaker has been embarrassed when not taking this into consideration!) Some are very sensitive to background noise, and some are not. Some may not have the volume set high enough, a problem often encountered when more than one person uses the same mike. An effective speaker needs to know if the mike is projecting her/his voice properly, and about the only way this can be accomplished is to ask the audience. If it seems inappropriate to ask them verbally, at least a speaker should nonverbally check by paying close attention to their eyes, whether or not they look like they're hearing what is being said. And if the speaker is speaking relationally, messages from the audience will be picked up. The second unfortunate assumption is that using a mike is a natural skill which doesn't need developing or practice. To be constantly aware of one's technologically projected voice takes some training. Just where on the clothing is the most effective placement of this or that lavaliere mike? Must I stick closely to the stationary mike, or will it pick up my voice at a distance; if so, what distance? Questions like these need to be addressed when using microphones. One wonders how speakers of old, like George Whitefield or John Wesley or Peter Cartwright or John Henry Newman, when speaking to large throngs of people, got their messages heard without the use of a public address system! Modern technology can increase our overall effectiveness as public speakers, but we need to know how to use it so it will not get in the way of the Message.

A Question of Style

Every public speaker/preacher will develop a distinctive style. Probably there are as many styles as there are speakers. Before we discuss the elements of style, it is useful to know just what it is. "Style," as I understand it, is very similar to how Jane Blankenship defines it in her text, *A Sense of Style* (Dickenson Publishing Co, Belmont, CA, 1968): one's "characteristic way of using the resources of the English language;" or as Stephen Ullman defines it (*Language and Style*, Barnes & Noble, NY, 1964): "primarily a personal and idiosyncratic mode of vision," or, maybe more simply put: "how someone characteristically communicates their vision of reality to someone else." Is it via repitition, or point-by-point organization, or by storytelling, or through animation in presenting their thoughts, or with humor, or by playing with or off the audience, or in the use of pauses and timing? Is one's style scholarly or back-woodsy? Is it self-disclosing and/or self-deprecating? Is it conversational or oratorical? Is it analytic? Is one's message filled with sarcasm or cynicism or is it just plain-talking? Does the person fill the message with sound-bytes or does it tend to be overly wordy? Are there some original, creative thoughts in one's speeches, or is it characteristically one cliche after another? Over a period of time these elements will coalesce into a distinctive style, one that will become as a "trademark" for an individual speaker. It is very interesting and insightful for speakers to identify their own styles. Then, as much as we sometimes wish we had another style, sort of "I'd like to be more like him or her in my speaking," we can concentrate on strengthening those elements in our own style so they can be more effective. It's the principle of "building on one's own strengths," rather than wishing to have someone else's strengths. Not everyone can be a successful big-city-church preacher. Not everyone can be a successful preacher in a crossroad's rural church. Styles differ. Our task is to identify and build on our stylistic strengths.

Nervousness: those "Butterflies" again!

Something needs to be said on the subject of "nervous tension." In almost every class I taught on public speaking, both at the university level and in workshops to other adults, one of the first and most intensely felt concerns of the students was their feeling of nervousness: "How do I get rid of my nervous tension?" My response, and the response of numerous other public speaking instructors, was (and is): "You don't; and you don't really want to." Nervous tension is not to be eliminated; it is to be managed. Why not work to eliminate this kind of discomfort? Because we all feel some nervous tension in public speaking situations. It's part of the human condition. As Henry Lambdin, my homiletics professor in seminary once said to his class: "If you get into the pulpit and your knees aren't shaking, look out; the Lord's not with you!" That was his way of saying that nervous energy is really a gift from God. Without it, speeches, especially sermons, often fall flat. With it, managed well, speeches, particularly those speaking the Word of God from the pulpit, generally fulfill their purpose. From the secular point of view, every public speaker experiences some level of nervousness, from the most famous speakers to the lesser known. It is just a natural phenomenon. How well we use this nervous tension is a question each of us must address.

An interesting survey, conducted in 1973, in which 2500 randomly selected Americans were asked what they most feared, the largest number of people (41%) listed "public speaking" as their number one fear. A far smaller number (18%) listed "death" as their number one fear. It seems that, for Americans at least, public speaking is more to be feared than death. Most of us have heard, in one way or another, the sentiment, "I'd rather do anything else than stand in front of a group of people and give a speech!" Why? Because it makes them too nervous. Strangely enough, some clergy often feel the same way, and spend an inordinate amount of time trying to get rid of it rather than to manage it and make it work for them. But how do we manage our nervous tension? By trial and error, mostly. The first step toward successful management has already been taken when the speaker acknowledges that s/he is experiencing a very common and natural phenomenon, one that everybody experiences at some level or other, whether or not they actually look nervous. Facing the unknown or a potential threat to one's self-image is always a frightening experience, and the human body naturally prepares itself to meet that potential threat by producing the protective chemical called "adrenalin." As we managed the adrenalin surge when we played competitive sports, or when we had our first date, or when we approached the altar to be married, so we can manage the adrenalin surge when we face the prospect of speaking in public. Once that step of acknowledging the naturalness of the nervous tension is taken, the speaker can employ any number of "excessive-tension managers," such as diet or food control, going off by oneself to focus on the task ahead (if, indeed, that works and the opportunity exists), convincing yourself that you know more about this specific subject than do your listeners (or that your perspective is both unique and valid), reminding yourself that your audience does not see all those signs of nervousness that you feel internally, using "visualization" as a tool for imagining success, making sure you're well rested and prepared, working hard on the introduction since that part of the speech sets the tone and establishes a positive relationship with the audience. Or other behaviors that will bolster self-confidence. Every clergy speaker needs to remember that some amount of nervous tension is a gift from God, given to us for many reasons, including both self-protection and to keep us from being so "cocksure" of ourselves that we fall into that spiritual trap of "thinking more highly of ourselves than we ought to think."

We Will Be At Least Partially Misunderstood!

Lastly, speakers need to remember that, try as we will, we cannot erase all possibility of being misunderstood. As I discussed in Chapter One, no matter how hard we try to be understood in our communication ventures, the normal result of the communication process is at least partial misunderstanding! It's no one's fault. It's just built into the very process. The most we can do, and the more effective speakers do it well, is to reduce the misunderstanding to a manageable level.

This discussion on public speaking and sermonizing is far from exhaustive. Much more can be said, and has been said in countless texts and classes. What I have tried to do in this chapter is only to highlight some of the aspects of public speaking that I think deserve special and ongoing attention by pastors as they approach this responsibility. If only one of my readers gains some insight into the speaking/preaching task, I will have accomplished my purpose in this chapter.

Chapter Fourteen
Four Specific Situations Demanding Special Communicating Skills

I chose to include the following four situations in a chapter of their own, not because they are the only types of interaction that deserve it, but rather because they are four interactions that seem to cause more than their share of problems for the pastoral communicator. I might have also included staff relationships, or communicating with the dying and their loved ones, or even communicating with little children. However, as much as these, and other, situations need addressing, too, space will not allow my zeroing-in on more than the four I have already identified. Hopefully, what I say here will show why they are so important in this chapter, and why, out of the host of situations in which a pastor must communicate, I chose to discuss these four. I imagine the other situations have been well addressed in other volumes; if this is not so, I may need to write an addendum to this chapter—sometime in the future.

Communicating in Power Situations

So the taskmasters and the supervisors of the people went out and said to the people, "Thus says Pharaoh, 'I will not give you straw. Go and get straw yourselves, wherever you can find it; but your work will not be lessened in the least.'" So the people scattered throughout the land of Egypt, to gathewr stubble for straw. The taskmasters were urgent, saying, "Complete your work, the same daily assignment as when you were given straw." And the supervisors of the Israelites, whom Pharaoh's taskmasters had set over them, were beaten, and were asked, "Why did you not finish the required quantity of bricks yesterday and today, as you did before?" NRSV Exodus 5:10-14

(Members of the Council) said, "What will we do with them? For it is obvious to all who live in Jerusalem that a notable sign has been done through them; we cannot deny it. But to keep it from spreading further among the people, let us warn them to speak no more to anyone in this name." So they called them and ordered them not to speak or teach at all in the name of Jesus. But Peter and John answeered them, "Whether it is right in God's sight to listen to you rather than to God, you must judge; for we cannot keep from speaking about what we have seen and heard." After threatening them again, they let them go, finding no way to punish them becaus of the people. NRSV Acts 4:16-21a

Whether it be in the Old Testament or the New Testament or in our modern world, all of us, at one time or another, will be communicating in a power situation—as the one with more of the power or as the one with less of the power. Since the presence of power has such a great impact on the process of communication, it is beneficial to understand this impact and look at ways it can be managed—toward the related goals of more effective communication and reducing the normal misunderstanding that will occur.

Whether the power is being expressed by physical coersion, as with the Pharoah's taskmasters, or by non-enforced threats, as with the Council members confronting Peter and John, it is still "power" (one person or group attempting to coerse another person or group to behave in a certain way which may or may not be accepted or chosen voluntarily by those being "pressured"). However, power is not always overtly expressed; it is often only perceived by one or both of the communicators, and that perception then becomes the basis for behavior. It is at this latter point that misunderstanding most often seems to occur. When power is obvious, options are few. But when power is only perceived (it may be real or it may be only imagined by one or both parties), many more possibilities exist for continued communication.

When power is obvious to both parties, communication

will occur in a dominant/submissive relationship. This does not mean we act as two dogs who have established a "pack-leader/pack submissive" relationship, where one is willing to roll over and present the vulnerable throat. It does mean that the mutual acceptance of the existing power will affect whatever goes on between the two individuals. This power-situation may be accepted by both, or by either one, or it may be resisted by both, or by either one.

I remember accepting a position as an Associate Pastor on a large church staff after I had spent five years being a successful Pastor in a couple of smaller churches. The Senior Pastor was in the "power seat;" we both perceived this and accepted it. He called and chaired the meetings. He assigned the pastoral duties (of course, with the approval of the pastor/parish committee). Even though we related as good friends, there was always the presence of power in our relationship. He would downplay it as much as he could, but I never could deny its existence. To paraphrase Harry Truman: "The buck stopped there." I perceived the power inherent in our staff relationship; and, I'm happy to say, we both managed it quite successfully.

Denominational structures also determine power relationships. In those churches where there is an ecclesiastical hierarchy, power tends to be located in the clergy. In those churches without an ecclesiastical hierarchy, power tends to be located in the lay people of the congregation. The pastor and the lay-people will most probably communicate in a somewhat different manner, depending on where the perceived power lay. Of course, there are churches that attempt to structure themselves with a "balance of power;" however, attempting to keep this balance of distributive power also affects the communication that occurs. (In simplest terms, people spend much time trying not to "step on each other's toes, or tred on the other person's turf.")

Not all power-relationships are accepted by the individuals involved. Sometimes, one person will resist any perceived attempt at communicating from a position of official or functional power. I was involved in a somewhat humorous (to me) situation at the university in which the Dean of the College sent a memo to all of the faculty reminding us that any change in time or place for the final exam period must be approved by the Dean. Since one of my upper division classes always had their final exam time at a local restaurant (the final exam itself was given earlier and the results shared right after the meal), I phoned the Dean for the required approval (he was exerting his power and I was accepting it). A surprise to me, he refused to give his approval (based on the weakest of all arguments: precedence). I gave him my reasons and (subtlely, I thought) challenged his authority to tell me how to teach my class. His response was a relinquishing of his power, in that he told me to do what I thought best to do, but he was not giving me permission to do so. His parting comment was: "Next time, Bob, just don't tell me." I wonder how many local pastors behave similiarly when functional "superiors" expect certain behaviors of them?

I do not mean to say, or even to imply, that the power relationship is something to be resisted or avoided in every situation. Not at all. Power can be a positive ingredient in any organizational structure, and sometimes serves a good purpose in interpersonal relationships. I only mean to say that its perceived presence will affect the communication relationship, and that this perception opens up numerous possibilities for interaction. It might be wise for a pastor to look beyond the obvious (and usually "official") power structure to the perceptions of power held by the individuals participating. "Where am I in this power-relationship? At what level is this other person perceiving my power in relation to her/him? What can I do to change this perception, if indeed it should be changed?" Answering these few basic questions can help to circumvent certain communication problems related to the subject of power.

As a final thought in this section on power, I would suggest that a rereading of chapters eight (on defensiveness) and nine (on conflict management) in Volume One might be very helpful.

Communicating Within the Organization

Moreover in Jerusalem Jehoshaphat appointed certain Levitges and priests and heads of families of Israel, to give judgment for the Lord and to decide disputed cases. They had their seat at Jerusalem. He charged them: "This is how you shall act: in the fear of the Lord, in faithfulness, and with your whole heart; whenever a case comes to you from your kindred who live in their cities, concerning bloodshed, law or commandment, statutes or ordinances, then you shall instruct them so that they may not incur guilt before the Lord and wrath may not come on you and your kindred. Do so, and you will not incur guilt. See, Amariah the chief priest is over you in all matters of the Lord; and Zebadiah son of Ishmael, the governor of the house of Judah, in all the king's matters; and the Levites will serve you as officers. Deal courageously, and may the Lord be with the good!" NRSV 2 Chronicles 19:8-11

Now during those days, when the disciples were increasing in number, the Hellenists complained against the Hebrews because their widows were being neglected in the daily distribution of food. And the twelve called together the whole community of the disciples and said, "It is not right that we should neglect the word of God in order to wait on tables. Therefore, friends, select from among yourselves seven men of good standing, full of the Spirit and of wisdom, whom we may appoint to this task, while we, for our part, will devote ourselves to prayer and to serving the word." NRSV Acts 6:1-4

The title of this section is purposefully misleading. Communication does not occur within the organization; it is the organization! You ask: "How can I say such a thing?" Consider: What is the purpose of organizing in the first place? Is it not to create a system for communicating? And why is such a system desired? Organizational theorists tell us that a communication system is created to accomplish a common goal. In an organization, communication is the process; accomplishment, the desired end-result. People systematize their communication in such a way as to most effectively achieve a desired goal.

Why did Jehoshaphat organize his people? So they could effectively communicate in order to live justly and peaceably with each other. Why did the twelve feel compelled to separate their serving of meals and serving the Word (organize by dividing up tasks)? So they could more effectively and efficiently communicate amongst themselves with less confusion and/or frustration, and communicate to the outside world with more time to do it and with less distraction. In both cases, as in numerous others in our scriptures, communication was at the heart (indeed, it was the very heart) of the organizing motivation. Without the systematized process of communication, there was no organization!

Therefore, when an organization is perceived as not operating satisfactorily, what we're really saying is that our communication process needs attention. Many's the time when members of an Organization, feeling frustration with themselves as a structured group because they are not satisfactorily fulfilling their commonly-held purpose, will spend time ad nauseum with models and charts in an effort to restructure. Rather than concentrate on their communication efforts that are working, given the personnel, culture, geographical area, history, and reward system in which they exist, and build on them, they design beautiful charts with all kinds of connecting lines that symbolize relationships that they want to create. They seek improvement by trying to squeeze people into little theoretical boxes, and expect them to behave like robots. When they don't, it's back to those infernal drawing boards.

Effective change in an Organization will occur when communication is improved, and not until then. Whether it be on the local church level or at a denominational level, humans must be held in higher regard than structure; human communication behavior must be considered before boxes and lines on a piece of paper!

Since Organizations are composed of people communicating with each other in order to accomplish some goal, and because together they can achieve goals that cannot be met as well by one person alone, given the fact that we are human beings with warts as well as wisdom, communication problems are unavoidable. Perceptions, and the motivations which emanate from them, will vary (as we discussed in Chapter Three) and create points of stress. Individual histories often create tension, which is expressed in the communicating that we do. Listening skills are often lacking. Defensiveness frequently raises its ugly head. Conflicts occur and few people are taught how to manage them satisfactorily. Status differences and pressures to conform are not unknown in an Organization. For all these reasons, and more, structural systems of communication (organizations) tend to experience cracks from time to time.

So how do we communicate more effectively within an organization, to use that misleading title? First and foremost, we accept the Faith-fact that every person in the Organization is exactly that: "a person; someone made in God's Image." Not a cog in an impersonal machine. Not a box or a line on someone's piece of paper. Not even a stereotypical "bureaucrat." Secondly, we accept the Faith-fact that those outside the Organization (of course, in this book I'm assuming the reader knows I am referring to the Church when I use the word "Organization" with a big "O") are also persons made in God's Image. They are not "clients," or "targets," or "potential converts," or any other label that categorizes them as objects. They are persons worthy of respect and relationship.

Thirdly, we will communicate more effectively by looking at the Organization as a "System for Communicating"—the Gospel, in this case. These acts of communicating are both verbal and nonverbal, spoken and acted-out. If "structure" or "design" seems more important than opportunities for communicating, if people interacting takes a back seat to boxes and lines and theories, the Organization is being counterproductive. It is not doing what it is meant to do: be an effective system for communicating. That is its reason for being! As long as communication can take place easily and effectively in a Formalized Structure (the Church as an Organization, both local and denominational), that Structure should be utilized to its capacity. Lines of communication, responsibility, and accountability are designed into the Organization for the purpose of enhancing interaction among human beings, not to be ends in themselves. When a line or a box on the Organizational Chart no longer fulfills the purpose of enhancing communication and sometimes even becomes somewhat of a barrier to communication, it needs to be jettisoned in favor of something that will. Of course, in as humane a way as possible. If, perchance, there is too much resistance to this kind of structural change, a resistance that could threaten the very life of the Organization, the people involved must (and will) find some informal way to communicate their message. Time and time again, people in organizations and Organizations have utilized the "grapevine" as their vehicle of choice. This is not the "gossip chain," as some have called it, although it can sometimes become that. The "grapevine" to which I'm referring is the informal system of relaying messages from person to person in hopes that decisionmakers will somehow "get the message" and do something about it. Responsible leaders will check the grapevine for messages as often as they check their e-mail for its messages.

One of the major problems in the Church as an Organization (any denomination will do for the example) is the uneasiness, and often unwillingness, to share our "failures" or "problems" with those most in the position to help us (because, of course, they can also "hurt" us). The pastor who admits such a problem or failure to someone within the Organization who has the power to punish and/or to reward is making him/herself very vulnerable. In a hierarchical Church, this position of power may be an official mentor or supervising pastor, a superintendent, or a bishop; in a non-hierarchical Church, this may be a member of the pulpit committee or the session or the administrative board. This is a variation on Rosen and Tesser's MUM effect (minimize unpleasant messages). And, yes, it often does come down to trust. We will trust the Organization that has made itself clear as to its use of power—that people come before structure in its decisionmaking and that effective avenues for communication not only exist but also are well-and-fairly-used. We will not trust any Organization with our vulnerability if it misuses the communication that is supposed to maintain that trust.

A central issue in any organization (with a little "o" or a big "O") is directional communication. I, personally, have a bit of trouble with two of the labels that are given to the directions. "Lateral communication" fits within my philosophy. "Upward" and "downward" do not. (So much so, that whenever a friend announces that s/he has been promoted to an administrative position, I ask them "Are you sure it isn't a demotion?") However, I don't have any substitute labels to offer that wouldn't confuse more than clarify; so I'll use them. Enhancing communication within an Organization includes a close look at all three directions to see that each is maintaining clear channels for listening and responding—and that they are being used. Is there regular and effective communication between committees and among individuals in the local church? Among local churches in the denomination? And with other Church bodies? (All called "lateral communication.") How about between the local clerics and the ecclesiastical hierarchy? Does this communication go as easily both ways? How about between the pastor and members of the congregation? ("Upward" and "downward" communication) Are both respected enough to be heard and responded to? Another important point of discussion: Are there adequate protections from attention-hogging time-wasters and harrassers (those who would misuse open channels of communication)? These and other questions will need to be weighed in any effort to enhance communication in any Organization.

Much more could be written here about communicating within an organizational structure. Books have been written about it: most for the secular business and corporate segment of our society; very little for the volunteer and non-profit segment; and almost none for the religious segment. It is up to us as churchpeople to apply what is relevant to us. This is what I have tried to do in as little space as possible, highlighting what I believe to be the more important starting points as we consider how to enhance our communication within our Organization: the Church.

Male/Female Communication

Then Delilah said to Samson, "How can you say, 'I love you,' when your heart is not with me? You have mocked me three times now and have not told me what makes your strength so great." Finally, after she had nagged him with her words day after day, and pestered him, he was tired to death. So he told her his whole secret. NRSV Judges 16:15-17a

When Boaz had eaten and drunk, and he was in a contented mood, he went to lie doen at the end of the heap of grain. Then she came stealthily and uncovered his feet, and lay down. At midnight the man was startled, and truned over, and there, lying at his feet, was a woman! He said, "Who are you?" And she answered, "I am Ruth, your servant; spread your cloak over your servant, for you are next-of-kin." He said, "May you be blessed by the Lord, my daughter; this last instance of your loyalty is better than the first; you have not gone after young men, whether poor or rich. And now, my daughter, do not be afraid, I will do for you all that you ask, for all the assembly of my people know that you are a worthy woman." NRSV Ruth 3:7-11

Male/Female communication: arguably the most discussed and written—about communication behavior in our society today—a topic that is steeped in emotion and very dependent on perceptions developed from individual histories. Even my above choices of Scriptural examples will draw the ire of some readers who will find in them communication problems that I do not at the moment see. Therefore, I write this section with real "fear and trembling," and with two books on my lap: Barbara Bate's *Communication and the Sexes*, and Judy Pearson's *Gender and Communication*. I encourage my readers to read these two information-laden books for a more complete understanding of this very important contemporary issue, especially as the topic of male/female communication relates to local church interaction and to the increasing number of women in the clergy.

Communication between the sexes is rife with stereotypes. Many of these stereotypes are reinforced by people acting in a way that they think our society expects them to act. Few are based on fact. Male/Female communication is a frequent cartoon topic: from Dagwood

& Blondie, to Hagar the Horrible, to B.C., to Caspar Milquetoast, to Peanuts, to Cathy, to Foxtrot, to For Better or Worse, ad infinitum. It must be true: that what we regularly laugh at indicates what is often of most concern to us. If we can chuckle over it, some of the sting of its truth or implication is easier to swallow.

As we consider Male/Female communication, by the title alone we are categorizing two distinct approaches to human interaction, plus a concern about the two approaches confronting each other, as if there really were male and female pigeon-holes into which we can place each person. There are those who quote research supporting the conclusion that males communicate out of the right hemisphere of the brain, while females integrate data from both sides of the brain in their communication. There are those who quote research supporting the conclusion that most of the communication of both males and females is culturally based, that we are socialized to communicate as males and females. Both ways of looking at it conclude that there are differences in the way we communicate, and that sex has something to do with it. However, the brain-development concluders say we can't do anything about it except live with it and adjust to it; while the socialization concluders believe that we can do something to change the way men and women communicate, and we do it by changing the way in which we socialize people. Of course, there are communicologists who try to ride both horses: that we can improve our socialization processes at the same time as we accept the biological differences and the limitations such differences force upon us—all the while accepting the fact that we communicate differently in some ways and that both ways seem to have strengths that the other does not have (or, in such abundance).

Now we bring the Church into the scene. Even though the Apostle Paul concluded that "there is no longer male and female; for all of you are one in Christ Jesus" (Galatians 3:28), I doubt that he was so naive as to believe all women would only communicate as he, a male, did. For whatever reason or combination of reasons, a number of differences

does exist in the way males and females communicate—
with members of their own sex as well as with members of
the other sex. And, yes, within the life of the Church as
well as outside of it.

My pastor is a woman. And I believe she's doing an
excellent job giving pastoral leadership to this fairly large
congregation. She's a superb preacher who liberally
sprinkles her sermons with arresting stories and
illustrations that appeal to males and females alike. I've
watched her relate to individuals on numerous occasions
in a manner that expresses love and concern, and a manner
that invites continued conversation and builds trust. Does
her gender make a difference in the way she communicates?
Possibly. Although I have observed males in the pastoral
role who behaved similarly. For a few months, both clergy
on our church staff were female. Did that create a fuss
among the church members? Not that I could tell. The
only comment I remember about that time was someone's
concern over the total absence of a male voice from our
liturgical leadership. However, I do not recall anyone being
concerned in the past over the total absence of a female
voice from the liturgical leadership. In a conversation with
a member of another church in another city, when I
mentioned my pastor (using the word "she"), I felt a shock
wave as my conversational partner reacted with utter
disbelief: "You don't have a woman pastor! That's not right!"
I must say that I was very grateful that this woman was not
in my congregation! Although, if she were (and she stayed),
I think she would have had her attitude soundly challenged,
and maybe would have changed her mind. At the moment,
we have a male Associate Pastor. Is it obvious from both
pastors' communication behavior that one is female and
the other male? Again, not that I can tell. They both have
their own communication style, and I would be hard pressed
to label one style as being male and the other, female.

What does all this mean? It means simply that the greater
share of my personal experience does not support most of
the gender-communication stereotypes I'm told we as a
culture have. Some may label me as naive because their

personal experience points to something else. However, wisdom dictates that I not depend solely on my own personal experience for my conclusions on any subject—and, in this case, gender communication. That is why I have two books on my lap.

Both authors either state clearly or imply that physical and social intimacy is oftimes imagined when males and females communicate on personal levels; of course, in our socialized culture, males seem to be more frequently interested in that kind of interaction, especially when they misinterpret the female tendency to communicate with relationship terminology, and the higher comfort level they seem to have when doing it. Such imagination and interest tends to cloud any communication that occurs between the sexes. It is another hurdle communicators must overcome; to insist that it does not exist is folly.

I found some aspects of gender-communication more intriguing than others; one particularly being the subject of "listening"—arguably the most important interpersonal skill of a pastor. It seems, by what both Bate and Pearson say, that men and women listen differently, and that one style is no better than the other; neither is superior to the other, only different. Men tend to select information that leads to a firm conclusion and a definite goal, something that will make logical sense when completed. Women tend to select data that confirms a pattern of "relatedness," and information which justifies intuitive perceptions, allowing emotions and unclear impressions much more influence on their conclusions than do most men. Pearson emphasizes that probably the "androgynous" individual is the most effective listener, in that s/he listens in both styles.

One area in gender-communication that creates very few disagreements is the topic of self-image or self-concept. We have definitely been socialized when it comes to what we think about ourselves. From the moment of birth, we are moulded into confident or less-than-confident human beings. Unfortunately, more females (and this seems to be true in many cultures) have been systematically persuaded to be less-than-confident than have males. The English language, which is fast becoming the universally understood language, gives a more positive slant on maleness than it does on femaleness. Generic pronouns are male; labels which categorize men are generally positive, whereas labels which categorize women are generally negative. Pearson quotes several studies of labeling and language usage that underscores women as being considered after-thoughts and second-class citizens in the English-speaking world. In Chapter Two of my first volume, I included an article by Theodora Wells which described in graphic terms what a man would feel like if all the things said about a girl as she was growing up were said about him as a young boy. He would feel powerless and unimportant. Our culture may be changing in this regard, but the studies to which Pearson and Bate refer seem to indicate it is not changing very fast or very much. And since everyone primarily communicates her/himself, if that self is considered unimportant or powerless, that negative self-image is what will be communicated to others. When the negative self-image (in a female) and the more positive self-image (in a male) interact, the result most frequently seen is a dominant/ submissive relationship—and this influences their communicating with each other. To counteract this consequence, we in the Church must continue to raise our people's awareness of both the cultural self-image problem and the language-usage problems we've discussed here, and provide more opportunities for women to become positive role models.

Barbara Bate, in writing about the intimate male/female relationship, states: "Three principles of equal relationship— integrity, reciprocity, and flexibility—suggest the values that can guide the communicative process for an intimate pair as they navigate together." (*Communication and the Sexes*, p.191) This is also true for us in the Church (clergy and laity alike). Integrity: through our communication behavior, honoring every other person, male and female, as being created in the Image of God and worthy of respect for their individuality and uniqueness. Reciprocity: communicating in a manner that seeks and receives positive responses, each continually taking into account the concerns of the other, accepting the validity of each other's experience and journey. Flexibility: acknowledging that change is inevitable and that no system of decisionmaking is flawless (the process of communication itself is flawed!), making adaptation necessary from time to time for relationships to function acceptably for all.

As I write and ponder the above, it strikes me that what I have described as beneficial for communication between the sexes will demand more change from the traditional male behavior than from the traditional style attributed to the female communicator. Each of these three values, especially the second and third, is closer in description and function to what has been traditionally assigned as feminine characteristics. Maybe it's time we changed the assigned labels: rather than male and female categories, to functional and dysfunctional, or to praiseworthy and unpraiseworthy, or to the style that enhances communication and the style that does not enhance communication!

As I stated earlier in the chapter, so much more could be included in each of these sections, especially in this one. My advice at this point is to find and read the works of people like Pearson and Bate, authors who have studied this subject for years, and writers without some "ax to grind," but who communicate a balanced and fair approach to this very volatile field of study.

Communication and Family Relationships

When the boys grew up, Esau was a skillful hunter, a man of the field, while Jacob was a quiet man, living in tents. Isaac loved Esau, because he was fond of game; but Rebekah loved Jacob. NRSV Genesis 25:27,28

When they did not find him, they returned to Jerusalem to search for him. After three days they found him in the temple, sitting among the teachers, listening to them and asking them questions. And all who heard him were amazed at his understanding and his answers. When his parents saw him they were astonished, and his mother said to him, "Child, why have you treated us like this? Look, your father and I have been searching for you in great anxiety." He said to them, "Why were you searching for me? Did you not know that I must be in my Father's house?" But they did not understand what he said to them. Then he went down with them and came to Nazareth, and was obedient to them. NRSV Luke 2:45-51a

When Jesus saw his mother and the disciple whom he loved standing beside her, he said to his mother, "Woman, here is your son." Then he said to the disciple, "Here is your mother." And from that hour the disciple took her into his own home. NRSV John 19:26,27

Our Scriptures allude to all kinds of family relationships—from the tension-filled home of Jacob, Esau, Isaac and Rebekah, to the child-parent adjustments of Jesus, Mary, and Joseph, to the breaking-apart and filling-the-void experience of Jesus and his mother. There's Adam & Eve & Cain & Abel, Abraham & Sarah & Hagar & Ishmael & Isaac, Ruth & Naomi & Boaz, Hosea & Gomer, James & John & Zebedee, Simon Peter & Andrew, Saul & Jonathan, David & Abigail & Bathsheba & Solomon & Absolom, etc., etc., etc.. Some of these Biblical relationships would be analyzed by contemporary psychologists as being functional, while others, very dysfunctional. Whatever the analysis, these are stories of family relationships, stories that are not irrelevant to the families of today.

Not only do pastors minister to families, they are also part of a family. And it is on this latter relationship that I wish to focus. Whether or not a pastor is single or married, whether a parent or not, s/he is still wedded to a family. Pastors have or had parents; most probably have or had siblings; some of us have nieces and nephews, uncles and aunts and cousins. We've had grandparents; at least some of us have been so fortunate. All of these relationships make or have made demands upon our attention and time. Hopefully, most of these relationships are pleasant ones; some, probably, are not. Some demand more attention than others. Geographical distance is a factor, especially in our mobile society. In light of all this, how does a pastor cope? How do we handle our family relationships?

To state the obvious, every situation is different. Families vary. Personalities differ. Pastors are not formed from the same mould. However, maybe there are a few generalized similarities worth considering here.

Married clergy may have different priorities than do unmarried clergy. The Roman Catholic priesthood has long struggled with this subject. It rightly acknowledges that a spouse and children will realign a pastor's priorities—at least the pastor's time commitments. Time must be spent relating to (communicating with) members of one's nuclear family. How much and when is negotiable. Some kind of balance must be struck between the demands of the parish and the demands of the family. The process of hammering this out, as well as the necessity of including some flexibility in it, takes careful and caring communication.

When I was in the pastorate, and my children were young, we (the parish council, my homemaker wife, and the children) decided that Monday would be set aside as "family day;" and we negotiated that most evening meetings which I was expected to attend throughout the week would begin at eight o'clock instead of seven or seven-thirty, so I could be with my children until they went to bed. Only funerals and life-or-death-emergencies would take precedence to family activities at these times. When the children were of school age, and my wife taught public school, Saturdays became my "day-off;" of course, with the same exceptions. This worked well for us; but I know of other pastors who worked a different schedule—and happily so. In each case, communication was the process by which they arrived at their schedule. Did ever a church member demand non-emergency attention when it was family-time? Oh, yes. I remember one time, in particular, when we were walking out the door to get in the car for a day at the lake, and the telephone rang. It was a longtime member of the church who demanded, in no uncertain terms, that I see her right away for she was going through an emotional crisis. I was in a dilemma, to be sure. But I had an obligation to my family, and this woman I knew was in a constant emotional crisis. I weighed the situation and told the woman that I would either call on her when I returned from the lake in the evening, or on the next day at her convenience. She became verbally abusive and hung up. I went to the lake with my family. And I called on her when I returned, only to find that the "emergency" had to do with the flowers which were scheduled to be on the altar on Sunday. Yes, I believe there are times when our family responsibilities conflict with our parish "duties;" but I do not believe every pastoral event should take precedence over our family-time opportunities. After all, what we communicate to our spouses and to our children needs to be considered as important, too—and maybe as much God's work as what we say to our church members.

This is not to say the unmarried or nonparent pastor never has this kind of dilemma with which to contend. Many pastors have parents still living, especially today with more people living longer, who need attention and care. Parishioners do not always understand that, particularly when they are emotionally distraught. It takes considerable interpersonal skill to meet the needs of both parents and parishioners at a time like that, without incurring a troublesome burden of guilt when the needs of both cannot be met at the same time. Church members who are served by a pastor who is single will often reason that since the pastor is unmarried, s/he doesn't have any family responsibilities and has all the time in the world to serve their spiritual needs. It takes much education to convince them otherwise, but convinced they must become for peace in the parish—and they will become more easily convinced when they are not suffering a personal "crisis."

When serving a church as pastor in a small midwestern city, my son, one day while making some pastoral calls, encountered an attitude I thought had been relegated to our rural past: "Didn't your wife come with you? Mrs. So-and-so always called with her husband, Rev. So-and-so." In our Protestant Church past, the spouse (almost universally the wife) oftimes assumed the role of "Assistant Pastor," being expected to call in the homes of the congregation, give leadership to the Ladies' Aid, play the organ and/or direct the choir, open the parsonage to all sorts of group meetings, be prepared to offer prayers at any gathering, and act as church secretary. My son, and countless other young pastors, needed to establish with the congregation the parameters for his family's involvement in church activities. Without mutually understood parameters, communication between pastor and people and between pastor and family can lead to unnecessary tension and conflict.

I've always been interested in the phenomenon we call "preacher's kid," although I never fit into that category since my father was a salesman. It seems to conjure up all kinds of images, mostly negative. A dominant image seems to be an undisciplined child who "can get away with murder"—someone whose behavior is in contrast to the "holiness" the preacher-parent is trying to get the congregation to emulate. Some "P.K.'s" do exhibit that kind of behavior, but, I would venture, far more do not. (A little known fact is that more 'preachers' kids" are in Who's Who in America than children of any other vocation. Although someone could reason that they "get it out of their systems early-on, then straighten up and fly right.") Whatever the reason for the stereotype, the pastor/parent will have numerous opportunities to reflect on it. One of my sons, when he was pre-school, enjoyed disrupting his Church School class on Sunday mornings by standing and running on the window-sill heating units. The teacher didn't want to tell me about it ("because I was the Pastor") and I didn't find out for a number of weeks and then only by someone else's slip-of-the-tongue. My son and I communicated about that, and he didn't do it anymore. I also needed to convince his teacher that it was doing a disservice to my son not to keep me informed of his misbehavior as well as his good behavior (of which she had much to say on the latter, thankfully). The pastor's children should not be treated any differently than anyone else's children—a message we need to get across to our congregations as well as to our family members. And (I expect to get some flak on this one): neither should we hold the pastor's children to any higher standard of behavior than we expect from other children in the congregation. Resisting the pressures to become models of behavior has "turned off" too many P.K.'s to the "Faith of their Parents."

I have always been a firm believer in married couples periodically "getting away by themselves" for a few hours or even a few days. This is just as true for the parsonage couple as it is for any other couple. A time apart for some serious adult conversation (a "date" if you will) is crucial for any young parents. And it is equally important as the family matures. Those lines of communication continually must be nurtured. As the pocketbook allows, sometimes the whole family needs to experience a different environment in order to appreciate each other more.

Families are important, and every member of our family needs to know that we pastors believe it enough to model it. All the sermonizing in the world will mean nothing if that sense of importance is not felt at home. And only caring communication will create and build that feeling of "family."

Chapter Fifteen

Ethics in Communication

Shadrach, Meshach, and Abednego answered the king, "O Nebuchadnezzar, we have no need to present a defense to you in this matter. If our God whom we serve is able to deliver us from the furnace of blazing fire and out of your hand, O king, let him deliver us. But if not, be it known to you, O king, that we will not serve your gods and we will not worship the golden statue that you have set up."   Daniel 3:16-18 NRSV

But while he (the Prodigal Son) was still far off, his father saw him and was filled with compassion; he ran and put his arms around him and kissed him. Then the son said to him, "Father, I have sinned against heaven and before you; I am no longer worthy to be called your son." . . . But he (the elder son) answered his father, "Listen! For all these years I have been working like a slave for you, and I have never disobeyed your command; yet you have never given me even a young goat so that I might celebrate with my friends. But when this son of yours came back, who has devoured your property with prostitutes, you killed the fatted calf for him!"
Luke 15:20,21,29,30 NRSV

When they had brought them, they had them stand befor the council. The high priest questioned them, saying, "We gave you strict orders not to teach in this name, yet here you have filled Jerusalem with your teaching and you are determined to bring this man's blood on us." But Peter and the apostles answered, "We must obey God rather than any human authority." Acts 5:27-29 NRSV

Toward a Definition of Communication Ethics

Who would have guessed that there would be a chapter on "ethics" in a book on communication for pastors? Yet here it is! And I think appropriately so. However, I hope the reader will not put down the book at this point and just anticipate that I will only reiterate what has already been said by numerous critics of our day as they view the contemporary scene. My perspective on the subject and my approach to it is anything but typical. You'll find no "shoulds" or "should-nots" coming from me in this chapter.

Coming from my behaviorist-influenced orientation, I do not look at ethics as a list of do's and don'ts, as an expression of standards agreed upon by executives or legislators of an organization or governmental body. Nor do I look upon them as a compilation of ideal behaviors which individuals in an organization are to exemplify or against which they are to be judged. Such listings and compilations of high-standards are "codes of ethics" and, I admit, do have their place in an organization and serve a worthy purpose, even so far as being integrated into some fraternal ritual; but "ethics" they are not.

"Ethics" are what we do. They are behaviors, not ideals. They are "acted out," not just something we hold in our minds. Ethics are behaviors, not principles. And, (here's where some of my critics cringe) since every human being behaves in some way, every human being is ethical! To call someone "unethical" because that person's code of conduct differs from ours is to misapply the term. Rather than label someone with such a negative word, we would be more fair and accurate to identify the ethical system by which that person operates—and then determine our own behavior in response to her/him. (Do we want to elect or appoint that person? Do we want to be in that person's audience week after week? Do we want to work with that person or be friends with that person? Do we want to follow or recruit that person to follow us?) People are "unethical" only when they behave in contradiction to their own normal and established behavior patterns. If the reader will stay with me, I will attempt to show how this way of looking at ethics has a practical application, especially for persons in vocations that require human interaction, and doubly so for those who are by definition cast into the "right vs. wrong" fray (clergy included).

I need to separate "communication ethics" from the broader and all-inclusive subject of "ethics" in general. By "communication ethics," I mean "the patterns of behavior with which we communicate with each other." It's "how we transfer and respond to intentional messages, be they verbal or nonverbal." I contend that we can identify these patterns, both in ourselves and in others, and the principles that create and drive them. In ourselves, once we identify the ethical framework by which we communicate, we can evaluate it according to the responses it receives and decide if it is to our liking or if we want to change it. Likewise, when we identify the ethical framework and patterns of communication by which others live, we can decide whether or not we wish to continue relating to them, or we can decide how to vary our own communication behavior in order to relate to them more effectively and comfortably. So there is, after all, a practical application to all this theoretical jargon and philosophical explanation.

Shadrach, Meshach, and Abednego all were ethical communicators. They lived a pattern of loyalty to their God and would not bow down to any golden image (a behavior by which they would be communicating loyalty and submission). Likewise, Nebuchadnezzar was an ethical communicator. His pattern, as king, seemed to be giving commands and expecting them to be obeyed. He communicated authority that was not to be questionned. The Prodigal Son "suddenly came to himself," and changed his communication behavior towards his father from self-determination and arrogance to one of repentance and humility. One might ask, "Was this a change of ethical framework or was this a 'strategy' of communication emanating from the same principle of self-centeredness?" The elder son's communication ethics may well have been the more consistent of the two: he expected just rewards (as he understood justice) and then grumbled about it when neither he nor his younger brother would be receiving them. The Prodigal's father communicated a relationship of indulgence toward his younger son in giving him his share of the property, then continued that indulgence in welcoming the boy back with such elaborate celebration. In stating that all that he had left belonged to the elder son, the father was behaving consistently as a "giving" person and implied that he was somewhat bewildered that the elder son didn't naturally know that. The elder son hadn't recognized the father's ethical framework of indulgence and the pattern of communication that resulted from it. The high priest, in our third Scriptural example, might be likened to Nebuchanezzar as a person communicating his authority over other people, as a person expecting to be obeyed. Simon Peter, on the other hand, was communicating his personal ethic: he must obey God rather than men, regardless of the consequences. Peter recognized the high priest's authority, but chose not to obey because he followed a higher authority, a belief that sustained a pattern of communication our tradition tells us lasted the rest of his life.

Communicologists over the years have described a number of ethical frameworks on which people base their communication behavior. In my teaching of communication ethics over the past twenty-some years, I have identified nearly one hundred fairly distinct frameworks, of which I will describe here fewer than a dozen as examples. (Because of the limited space in this chapter and book, for those readers who wish a more in-depth exploration of communication ethics, I suggest reading Richard Johannesen's *Ethics In Human Communication*, 3rd edition, and/or Jim Jaksa's *Communication Ethics: Methods of Analysis*. Although I prefer Johannesen's overall approach, both of these paperbacks will fill in most of the gaps in this chapter.)

Legal Perspectives

Some people operate from a legal perspective, holding that laws are primarily ethical principles written into society's regulations by some kind of legislative action. The First Amendment to the United States Constitution is an example of this: all citizens are guaranteed the freedom to speak their minds. It's the law! (With a few exceptions as decided by our court system. Of course, these few exceptions have become the law, too—by both judicial and legislative action.) Restricting anyone's freedom of expression (with those few exceptions) is unethical communication behavior; conversely, creating an atmosphere in which people can express themselves freely would be termed as ethical communication behavior. Someone would be deemed ethical when applying this principle to all phases and levels of life, in the parental role as in the workplace role, or the religious role. Once a law or rule has been made, all behavior relating to that issue must be measured by that standard. As Johannesen describes this aspect of the legalist's perspective: "truth is that which is not legally false." Or, to state it another way: right behavior is that which is not specifically prohibited by the law. The strict Pharisee of Biblical times communicated from a legal perspective, only justifying that communication which was approved in their tradition. Even the inflexible Biblical literalist of modern times might be labeled a legalist—one who bases all behavior, including communication, on the literal understanding of Scripture: if the Bible (our religious law book) doesn't speak against it, then it's OK to do. Anything not recorded as evil is not evil. A religious legalist might be one who bases all behavior on the Ten Commandments, only doing what they allow, and not doing what they do not allow. There are many brands of ethical legalists, both in the clergy and in the laity. And not only in the Judeo-Christian traditions; our Muslim brothers and sisters in the Middle East and North Africa know them only too well.

Utilitarian Perspectives

Another perspective-category is one based primarily on the workability of an approach, one that is not tied to a specific ideological principle other than one of usefulness, pleasure, and happiness. Johannesen describes this approach in the form of a question: "Does the technique or goal promote the greatest good for the greatest number in the long run?" Of course, such an approach is not altogether separated from an ideological principle: the meaning of "greatest good," which may be rooted in some other perspective. The communicator who operates from this perspective will regularly apply to her/his words the question: "Will my words (or silence) benefit the greatest number of people?"

William Howell developed what he labeled "The Social Utility Approach." In this perspective each communicator has an "Ethical Quotient" or "EQ" (much like an Intelligence Quotient or IQ), in that s/he holds a certain high standard for behavior that ideally s/he will exhibit with few exceptions. Given most situations, this person will behave in a certain manner, according to her/his "EQ." But—situations may arise and circumstances may occur when this personal ideal does not necessarily benefit the greatest number of people or the greater number of people affected and/or involved. Then the person will apply this latter (utilitarian) principle, that the benefit to the larger society is more important than the personal ideal. This implies that a society's created basic value system (which has been developed over time by the people involved) will be preserved. Whatever communication supports the cultural values of a society is considered ethical, and whatever communication tends to weaken it or damage it is to be considered unethical. Thus, for Howell, ethics (including communication ethics) is both culture-specific and a "function of context."

Human Nature Perspectives

What makes a human-being human? What sets the human apart from the rest of the animals? Is it the capacity to reason? or the ability to use symbols? or is it conscience? or the use of language? or the ability to persuade? or the drive to seek and/or create Truth? The answer to each of these questions emanates from some ethical framework, and will affect the way a person communicates.

Aristotle receives credit for lifting "rationality" to new heights as that which makes a human-being truly human. This is not to say the great philosopher did not acknowledge the power of emotion and the necessity of employing it judiciously. His view of rhetoric was to use all available means of persuasion. From my reading I've come to the conclusion Aristotle looked at ethical communication as either (or preferably) a balance between reason and emotion, or as more reason than emotion; but never as primarily emotion. Too much emotion (or appeals to our animal instincts) in one's communication would have been unethical to Aristotle.

Others have built on Aristotle's view and added their own unique observations and conclusions. For example, a person is more human (therefore more ethical) when acting more reflectively than spontaneously; or when operating more in the realm of logic than speculation; or when behaving and helping others to behave rationally rather than emotionally; or when respecting the cognitive processes of self and others. A person operating from this framework would not look favorably upon the modern practices of advertising with its emphasis on emotive stimulation. Neither would s/he be comfortable sitting in the pew listening to a highly emotive preacher.

Immanuel Kant's "Categorical Imperative" gives us another view of human nature that impacts on communication behavior. A "sense of conscience," a universal moral will or reason, a general sense of right and wrong, is an inherent and unique characteristic of every human being. These moral imperatives are categorically "right." Operating (communicating) outside these imperatives would be considered unethical behavior. For example, telling the truth is a universal law, and anyone who lies for whatever reason is being unethical—unless s/he can honestly justify the lie by a willingness to have such behavior become a universal law. Without such justification that everyone should lie in similar circumstances, that communication is considered unethical.

Another interesting framework within this general category has been described by Robert Scott of the University of Minnesota. He views human beings as creators of truth—this ability being what differentiates a human being from an animal. It is through human communication (interaction) that Truth is created. To withdraw from this process of dialog, of creating, is to be unethical. Tolerating divergent viewpoints and supporting the right of expression for self and others are basic to Scott's ethic, for it is only by doing so that truth becomes possible—and is created.

Political Perspectives

By "political perspectives" I mean those perspectives that are rooted in a society's fundamental principles regarding the rights of communicators and the processes of expression. In the United States of America, these principles are found in the Constitution, and particularly in the First Amendment (of course, as interpreted by our court system!). Freedom of Speech is one of our most cherished freedoms, and is the foundation of our entire democratic system.

A number of thinkers ground their communication ethics in their understanding of what it means to be a citizen of a free-speech democracy. Thomas Nilsen labels his perspective "Significant Choice." Decisions are to be made in an atmosphere of open communication in which there is free, informed, and critical choice, particularly in matters that are significant to the participants. This choicemaking must be voluntary and free from any kind of coersion and based on the best and most complete information available at the time of the decision. The ethical is that which preserves and strengthens the process of democratic choicemaking. The unethical is that which weakens this process or demeans the choicemakers (all or any part of the democratic citizenry). This is an ethic rooted in democratic ideals.

Dennis G. Day's communication ethics is also grounded in the democratic process, but with a slightly different twist. Decisions are ethical only when arrived at by democratic means, whatever those decisions are. His is a procedural ethic. For him, a democratic society is defined by the method of decisionmaking—even to the point of downgrading the importance of reason, for as he says, "The ethics of democratic discourse require a commitment to debate, not a commitment to reason." (*Central States Speech Journal* 17, p.9) A democracy does not impose its values on the whole, but rather provides a procedural framework within which each citizen can actualize her/his own pursuit of happiness. To be unethical is to step outside this procedural ethic.

In a more totalitarian-governed society, the opposite point of view is the more accepted perspective on communication ethics. The monarch, the party chief, the religious leader, anyone who claims total jurisdiction over others, will hold a different ethical perspective than the one either Nilsen or Day hold, probably one which justifies subverting accuracy and truth in communication to the ruler's desires and position. Totalitarian leaders are ethical, too; they just do not adhere to the same understanding of communication ethics.

Relational Perspectives

I will briefly review only two relational perspectives: dialogical and existentialist. Even though both seem to approach relational communication from different directions, they arrive nearly at the same point.

Dialogical communication is probably best described in Martin Buber's classic work, *I and Thou*. The ethical person will relate to the other as a "Thou," a human being, not as an "It." The unethical person will relate to the other person as an object, an "It." Dialogical communication is identified by the attitude one person has toward the other. Viewing the other person as someone who can be used, as someone to manipulate, as someone to objectify, is monological behavior, an unethical act of communication.

Some of the people whose names are associated with the dialogical perspective are, besides Buber: Carl Rogers, Sidney Jourard, Abraham Maslow, Eric Fromm, Paul Tournier, Reuel Howe, John Powell, and Ashley Montagu. That which is created between human beings is the significant behavior in life. The more ethical "betweenness" is characterized by mutuality, honesty, absence of pretense (authenticity), and concern for the other's well-being. Buber emphasized, and most of the others named above confirmed, that "seeing the other side" is essential to dialogue. Rogers emphasized "empathic understanding" and applied it to his therapeutic work. Part of the dialogical framework is an "unconditional positive regard" for the other person, and seeing that person as one worthy of genuine respect.

When that "betweenness" exhibits coersion, manipulation, control, deception, or exploitation, we witness monological communication. A "monologist" will use a listener's feedback only to further her/his own purposes; thus, feedback becomes a tool for control used by a person who considers her/himself superior to the other. To persons who operate from a dialogical perspective, monolog is unethical communication.

If we could separate what has come to be known as the "existentialist" approach to life from Buber and the other dialogists (a difficult separation to make, to be sure), we could witness another slightly different relational perspective in communiction ethics. (Truth is, I could develop an argument for placing the existentialist perspective, besides here, in a number of perspective categories, particularly in the Human Nature category [where Johannesen places it] and in the Religious Perspective, next to be discussed.) The name of Jean-Paul Sartre is most frequently associated with the existentialist point of view. Individualism, in the sense of human beings as separated from one another, and freedom are the two bywords of this perspective. Language is to be used to connect these separated human beings, while at the same time fostering their freedom to perceive and choose. Complete certainty is impossible, so Sartre as an agnostic/atheist claimed, and the only truth is that which is perceived by the individual, but even then only tentatively. The ethical communicator is the person who employs language to connect these separated individuals while, at the same time, respecting their right to freedom. The unethical communicator is the person who employs language in such a way as to inhibit freedom, or to break the tentative connections between individual human beings as they struggle to live in a chaotic world.

Religious Perspectives

Finally, I come to the religious perspectives. It would be simple, but misleading, to assume that all readers of this book would be communicating from this perspective category. It would be absolutely naive to assume that all of our parishioners do. Since many of us within the religious community often claim the subject of ethics to be one of our specialized concerns and that it is our God-given right to define them and set their parameters, we have indeed defined a number of frameworks based on our religious beliefs and values. To describe all of them would be impossible; even to list all of them, difficult. Therefore, I will look at only a few of them as examples and for contrast.

The first sounds like it should be included in the next section rather than in this one: Joseph Fletcher's "Situation Ethics." Thirty years ago, his book by the same title created a stir in many a congregation. It sounded like Fletcher was endorsing an ethical system in conflict with Christian teachings. But a closer and more reflective appraisal of situation ethics convinces a reader that Fletcher was describing something quite different. His "bottom line" was "love"—as Christian concern for the welfare of other people. He described his understanding of Christian ethics in words to this effect: "If you can love another person by obeying the Ten Commandments, for example, then obey them; if you can only love that person by breaking one of the Commandments, then break it." One's ethical behavior is determined by the application of Christian Love to any situation. Rules, laws, regulations, customs, dogmas—all must be subjugated to Christian Love, and jettisoned if they're in the way of its application.

Adding the name of Kierkagaard to the philosophy of existentialism creates something which has been labeled "Christian Existentialism." The focus is on the here and now, on what is being created in a particular place at a particular time and among the people present. Both the past and the future are relevant only as they impact on the present moment. I, a Child of God, am only ethical in my communication with others, who are also made in the Image of God, when I am creating and sustaining a desireable relationship with them. I will respect their separateness even as I attempt, with the lifelines of love and language, to bridge the chasm between us. To do otherwise is unethical behavior.

Emory Griffin describes an ethic for Christian evangelism with the help of the "lover" metaphor. In observing the communication practices of Christian lover-persuaders, Griffin separates the ethical from the unethical. The true lover (the ethical) is both loving and just, caring for others more than for one's own ego, and respecting the rights of others (including the right to say "no"). There are a number of false lovers (the unethical), including the flirt (who sees souls as something to be counted), the seducer (who uses deception, flattery, and irrelevant appeals to entice an audience), the rapist (who uses psychological and emotional coersion to force a commitment), the smother-lover (who overwhelms others with love somewhat in a maternalistic manner, believing s/he knows what is best for everyone, thereby denying their uniqueness), and the legalistic lover (who persuades out of a sense of obligation or duty, not from the heart).

Some church denominations have set down certain

communication rules which they expect to be followed by their clergy. As I stated earlier, these are imposed expectations and codes of ethics, statements and positions developed by the general bodies against which clergy may be evaluated and judged. They are not necessarily the ethics which drive the clergy to act as they do. Clergy may accept one of these codes as their own; that is their choice. (However, as I reflect on this, when pastors use the denomination's code of communication conduct to justify their own behavior, such an act might place the pastor in the Legalistic Perspective!)

Situational Perspectives

Now we come to a perspective-category that many people automatically think is the perspective that is most prevalent in our contemporary Western world. It might be worded in a phrase we hear all too often: "It depends upon the situation." When my students would lay this phrase on me, my response was usually to ask a couple of very pointed questions: "Are you saying you have no values, no principles to guide your behavior? Do you really think you're intelligent enough to take every single element of differing situations into consideration when you are interacting with someone?" If every situation demands a different standard, if there are no abiding principles by which to act, if no one can count on a response somehow connected with some past behavior, we will be living amongst people who make decisions and establish relationships simply by the wiles and whims of each moment.

The name most often associated with this perspective is Saul Alinsky. His "Rules for Radicals" outlines his communication ethic. Among these "rules" we find justification for lying, if it will achieve one's goal—the end justifying the means. He contends there are no rules of fair play in war, and that in the battles for social justice, it is not unlike a war. Success is the major evaluator of ethical behavior. "You do what you can with what you have and clothe it in moral garments." He advises his radicals to use ridicule, as it is man's most potent weapon. He recommends as a tactic to "pick the target, freeze it, personalize it, and polarize it."

Edward Rogge described another approach to "situational ethics." Essentially, he suggested as ethical, only communication which was expected and/or believed and/or approved by the immediate audience, be that an audience of one, ten, or a thousand. Anything else was unethical.

As the reader can readily see, neither Alinsky nor Rogge are "pure situationalists." The abiding principle of Alinsky is to succeed by whatever method and at whatever cost. Once the principle is understood, and the goal is set, the means are determined by the situation. The abiding principle of Rogge is to respond to the audience's desires and their standard of acceptability. Once the principle is understood, and the audience is analyzed, the means (content and delivery) is selected to appeal to the audience, whether or not the speaker believes in what s/he says. The means are determined by the situation: communicating with that particular audience.

The pastor who understands her/his work as warring with Satan and battling the forces of evil, might also decide to break relations with certain of her/his congregation because of their evil ways, or tell a falsehood to further the conversion process of a parishioner. Communicating in this manner aligns the pastor with Alinsky, who advocates that as in war, the end justifies the means. If the pastor patterns her/his communication after Rogge's perspective, the congregation would only hear what they already believed, approved, or expected in the situation and at the given point in time.

So What?...

Most people, with reflection, can place their own communication behavior into one of the above perspective-categories. They can then decide if that is the perspective they wish to drive their communication with others; and for the pastors, if that is the perspective God wants them to have and express. If so, fine; they have additional understanding of who they are. If not, they can attempt to change their perspective, or at least take some steps in that direction.

By understanding that the people of the parish, whom they are to serve, members and nonmembers, will exhibit communication emanating from various ethical frameworks, the pastor should be able to work with them more effectively. Little by little, over the years, the pastor will be more able to affect changes in their worldview, which in turn will encourage them to change their ethical framework, if needed, to one more compatible with the Faith they hold. At the very least, the pastor who understands that one's communication behavior stems from one's ethical framework—and what some of those frameworks are—will be in a better position to help others understand themselves more fully, as well as the process and consequences of their own communication behavior.

Postscript to Volume Two

As a final word, having now completed these two volumes after many years of incubation, I must admit that I'm relieved. On these more than four hundred pages, not only have I discussed what I wish I had known during my first thirteen years as a young pastor, but also, in doing so, I have exposed much of myself with the illustrations chosen. As writers have done over the centuries, I have made myself vulnerable. My readers know much more about me than otherwise would have been known. Self-disclosure is often a frightening experience; but, as I wrote in Chapter Seven, it can also be a very rewarding one.

Now that the writing is finished, do I dare reread it all and probably discover that in many places I did not say what I had intended to say, and in many places I did say what I did not intend to say? No, I'll let it rest, hoping my readers will recognize this apprehension as part and parcel of George Shapiro's 4th generalization: "The normal result of the communication process is at least partial misunderstanding."

Sources & Acknowledgments

Chapter Ten

Garner, Alan. *Conversationally Speaking*. (New York: McGraw Hill, 1980).
Goss, Blaine & Dan O'Hair. *Communicating in Interpersonal Relationships*.
    (New York: Macmillan Publishing Company, 1988).
Weaver, Richard L. II. *Understanding Interpersonal Communication*, 5th ed.
    (Glenview, Illinois: Scott Foresman/Little, Brown Higher Education,
    1990).

Chapter Eleven

Adler, Ronald, Lawrence Rosenfeld & Neil Towne. *Interplay: The Process of
    Interpersonal Communication*, 5th ed. (Fort Worth, Texas: Holt, Rinehart
    and Winston, Inc., 1992).
Buber, Martin. *I and Thou*, 2nd ed., Trans., Ronald Gregor Smith. (New York:
    Scribners, 1958).
DeVito, Joseph. *The Interpersonal Communication Book*, 4th ed. (New York:
    Harper & Row, Publishers, Inc., 1986).
Duck, Steve, ed. *Dissolving Personal Relationships*. (New York: Academic
    Press, 1982).
Fisher, Aubrey. *Interpersonal Communication: Pragmatics of Human
    Relationships*. (New York: Random House, 1987).
Giffin, K. & B.R. Patton. *Fundamentals of Interpersonal Communication*.
    (New York: Harper & Row, Publishers, Inc., 1976).
Goss, Blaine & Dan O'Hair. *Communicating in Interpersonal Relationships*.
    (New York: Macmillan Publishing Company, 1988).
Hopper, Robert & Jack Whitehead, Jr. *Communication Concepts and Skills*.
    (New York: Harper & Row, Publishers, Inc., 1979).
Hybels, Saundra & Richard L. Weaver, II. *Communicating Effectively*. (New
    York: Random House, 1986).

Krayer, K. & Dan O'Hair. "The Development of a Typology of Reconciliation Strategies." (Unpublished manuscript, 1986).

Meyers, Gail & Michele Tolela Myers. *The Dynamics of Human Communication: A Laboratory Approach*, 5th ed. (New York: McGraw-Hill Book Company, 1988).

Chapter Twelve

Bormann, Ernest G. *Discussion and Group Methods*. (New York: Harper & Row, Publishers, Inc., 1969).

Fisher, Aubrey. *Small Group Decisionmaking: Communication and the Group Process*. (New York: McGraw-Hill Book Company, 1974).

Chapter Thirteen

Blankenship, Jane. *A Sense of Style*. (Belmont, CA: Dickenson Publishing, 1968).

Ehninger, Douglas, Alan H. Monroe, & Bruce E. Gronbeck. *Principles and Types of Speech Communication*, 8th ed. (Glenview, Illinois: Scott, Foresman, 1978).

Trueblood, Elton. *The Humor of Christ*. (New York: Harper & Row, Publishers, Inc., 1964).

Ullman, Steven. *Language and Style*. (New York: Barnes & Nobel, 1964).

Chapter Fourteen

Bate, Barbara. *Communication and the Sexes*. (New York: Harper & Row, Publishers, Inc., 1984).

Fisher, Dalmar. *Communication in Organizations*. (St. Paul, MN: West Publishing Company, 1981).

Hanna, Michael & Gerald Wilson. *Communicating in Business and Professional Settings*. (New York: Random House, 1984).

Pearson, Judy. *Gender and Communication*. (Dubuque, IA: Wm C. Brown Publishers, 1985).

Chapter Fifteen

Jaksa, James & Michael Pritchard. *Communication Ethics: Methods of Analysis*. (Belmont, CA: Wadsworth Publishing Company, 1988).

Johannesen, Richard L. *Ethics in Human Communication*, 3rd ed. (Prospect Heights, IL: Waveland Press, Inc., 1990).